7 MYTHS ABOUT WOMEN AND WORK

CATHERINE FOX is deputy editor of *Financial Review BOSS* magazine and writes a weekly column, 'Corporate Woman', for the *Australian Financial Review*. She joined the newspaper in 1989 and has held a variety of positions, including marketing and Smart Money editor, and court reporter. Before becoming a journalist she worked in financial services marketing and consulting in Sydney and London. She has worked for a range of organisations, including two of Australia's largest banks, a university and an advertising agency. Catherine has written two books, *The F Word: How we learnt to swear by feminism* with Jane Caro, and *Better than sex: how a whole generation got hooked on work* with Helen Trinca. Her journalism has won several awards, and she is a regular speaker at forums around the country. She is a member of several advisory bodies, and in early 2012 was appointed to the Defence Force Gender Equality Advisory Board. Catherine has a BA Communications (UTS) and MA Hons (UNSW) and lives in Sydney with her husband and three daughters.

7 MYTHS ABOUT WOMEN AND WORK

CATHERINE FOX

NEWSOUTH

A NewSouth book

Published by
NewSouth Publishing
University of New South Wales Press Ltd
University of New South Wales
Sydney NSW 2052
AUSTRALIA
newsouthpublishing.com

National Library of Australia Cataloguing-in-Publication entry

Author: Fox, Catherine (Catherine Louise)
Title: 7 myths about women and work / Catherine Fox.
ISBN: 9781742233475(pbk)
      9781742241173(epub)
      9781742243757(kindle)
      9781742246062(ePDF)
Subjects: Women executives – Australia.
      Women middle managers – Australia.
      Women – Employment – Australia.
      Businesswomen – Australia.
      Sex discrimination in employment – Australia.
Dewey Number: 331.481658400994

Design Josephine Pajor-Markus
Cover design Xou Creative
Printer Griffin Press

CONTENTS

For Simone, Evelyn and Antonia

ACRONYMS

ABS   Australian Bureau of Statistics
ACLW   Australian Centre for Leadership for Women
AICD   Australian Institute of Company Directors
APPEA   Australian Petroleum Production and Exploration Association
AWALI   Australian Work and Life Index
AWCCI   Australian Women Chamber of Commerce and Industry
BCA   Business Council of Australia
CAMAC   Corporations and Markets Advisory Committee
CEDA   Committee for Economic Development of Australia
CEW   Chief Executive Women
EOWA   Equal Opportunity for Women in the Workplace Australia (renamed Workplace Gender Equality Agency from March 2013)
FaHCSIA   Department of Families, Housing, Community Services and Indigenous Affairs

FINSIA	Financial Services Institute of Australia
GFC	Global financial crisis
HBR	Harvard Business Review
HREOC	Human Rights and Equal Opportunity Commission (renamed Australian Human Rights Commission)
MBA	Master of Business Administration
MBS	Melbourne Business School
MCC	Male Champions of Change
NATSEM	National Centre for Social and Economic Modelling
NFAW	National Foundation of Australian Women
ROE	Return on Equity
WiBF	Women in Banking and Finance
WOB	Women on Boards

ACKNOWLEDGMENTS

Many thanks to all those who have inspired and helped me in my myth-busting: *Financial Review* colleagues Rose Ann Manns, Fiona Smith, Narelle Hooper, Judith Hoare, Haki Crisden, Fiona Carruthers, Pam Williams; and the continuing conversations with Geraldine, Roger and Brendan Fox, Rosemary Johnston, Jane Caro, Margot Saville, Adele Miles, Michele Jackson, Aviva Lowy, Michael Visontay, Meredith Brooks, Helen Connealy, Arlene Tansey, Miriam Silva, Ruth Medd, Claire Braund, Frances Feenstra, Elizabeth Broderick, Anne Summers, Hannah Piterman, Wendy and Sophie McCarthy, Carol Schwartz, Kate O'Reilly.

Thanks also to Phillipa McGuinness, Kathy Bail and Uthpala Gunethilake at UNSW Press and *Financial Review* Group CEO Brett Clegg. And of course to my nearest and dearest: David, Simone, Evie and Antonia.

INTRODUCTION:
WHY 7 MYTHS?

When Margaret Whitlam died in early 2012 several tributes described her as a woman of many attributes, with a great sense of humour, who was very much at ease with herself. At her funeral the eulogies made the point that she had been confident enough to be simply who she was – not a 'first lady' prototype or a female consort from central casting, but an intelligent, self-possessed woman on an equal footing with her husband, former Prime Minster Gough Whitlam. In an era when most married women's lives centred on the home, Margaret Whitlam carved out a valuable public role for herself in a particularly traditional space.

It sounds deceptively simple in hindsight, but such equilibrium and strong sense of identity are still rare things to observe in women, even today. Our gender continues to define and contain us in ways that are complex, frustrating and often defy commonsense. And that's why a century after women won the vote in this country and started the hard task of dismantling the barriers to fully participating in society, there is still a pressing need to examine the mythology about being female in the workforce.

This is not a book about how to be Margaret Whitlam, but it is about understanding why there are many reasons women continue to confront a series of perplexing and often contradictory ideas and assumptions about how they live their lives, the roles that are deemed acceptable for them in society and in the world of paid work. You will not find conspiracy theories or unhelpful 'he said, she said' debates here, but lots of information about human nature and behaviour in hierarchies that have allowed fundamental misconceptions to flourish. These myths are perpetuated in the business world because they are comfortable and the way things have operated for decades – indeed, in some cases, for centuries. In fact, it was after hearing a few of them stated with great conviction by a CEO I interviewed for the *Financial Review* that the 7 myths idea took shape. I realised the conversation had a familiar ring and I'd heard the same old, irritatingly inaccurate excuses for the lack of women in business, the gender pay gap and other problems trotted out time and again by senior executives of both sexes. A couple of my workmates suggested (probably to stop my rant) that I make a list and write it up for the 'Corporate Woman' column. It seemed like a good idea and a rather elegant way of covering off on a few of my main bugbears. So the list of 7 myths was born.

It quickly became apparent that the column had struck a chord. Just as I found the 7 myths format a useful shorthand for communicating some of the enduring themes I noticed in my work on this area, so it seemed my readers found it a handy way of summarising a lot of the trends, misunderstandings and frustrations they noticed in their workplaces. They told me the column helped to get their thoughts in order and also provided ammunition for those informal workplace conversations that actually carry a lot of weight and influence attitudes. The feedback kept coming in, as well as quite a few invitations to speak about the myths at conferences and businesses around Australia. On every occasion I found the discussion yielded even more evidence that the myths needed dismantling.

These ideas were obviously remarkably tenacious, and not just among men, with many women telling me they had absorbed some of the generalisations about their gender and never really stopped to analyse or test them against actual experience. Most of the myths have survived in the face of strong evidence to the contrary, as we shall see.

As I pursued my myth-busting mission it was apparent there was a consciousness-raising element to this exercise that I had never thought would prove so potent and gratifying. The faltering progress towards better gender equity in all sorts of sectors had left many women worn down and despondent. Yet puncturing the myths did not seem to add to that effect, but, according to most of my feedback, provided more of a confidence booster by offering some ways to actively counter this unhelpful discourse.

After a period of glacial change, and a backsliding in some indicators, it's not all bad news at the coalface these days. Some progress towards a fairer workplace has begun after a long period of inertia during the first decade of this century, although much of it is about catching up. It builds on some of the major steps made to provide women with the same opportunities as men in the workforce over many decades: we no longer have a marriage bar in the public service, women are not forced to resign when they have children, there's paid maternity leave and the right to flexible work is becoming more widespread. But we cannot ignore the many inequities that still affect women in all sorts of jobs, despite many years of solid economic growth in Australia and plenty of effort to generate some action.

Australia is not alone. Many developed economies have registered sluggish progress along the path to better gender equity over the last few years. There are many reasons – social, historical, economic, organisational and behavioural – and most will be examined as I analyse the myths. But it is also clear to me that this is not because women see no need for change or have given up after many tussles for a fair go, nor that the men still dominating management ranks of business have formed a conspiracy to block equity measures. It's more a combination of passive resistance and the defence of the status quo, driven by fear of change, rather than concerted objection.

It's a hard nut to crack. The surge of women into the workplace while they remain stuck with the primary domestic role means that most of us have a daily 'to do' list of daunting proportions that leaves us exhausted. Storming the barricades for equal rights or even turning up to another diversity discussion can fall down the priority list when a job deadline approaches and you have to be out of the office by 5.30 pm to pick up the kids. And it's not as though our male peers or managers have exactly encouraged the discussion or even acknowledged that there is a genuine problem.

We have a way to go before that is achieved, according to Australian academic Dr Hannah Piterman in *Women in Leadership*:

> Despite the clear business case backed by
> extensive research that has aligned improved
> financials and healthier, more positive cultures
> with the increase of women at senior ranks, the
> gender parity chasm still exists. Not only are

women excluded from the leadership table, but they are held to account for being women.

The business case for gender equality is clear but the solutions are complex. Gender diversity is by no means unanimously accepted as a strategic priority. Perceptions of its importance vary, particularly between men and women ...

The resulting dynamic sees women having to prove that they are extraordinary. That they are without needs or demands, and that they are unencumbered by family in order to avoid being sidelined as less ambitious, as not having the prerequisite experience and of not wanting to commit.

This is one tall order if you don't happen to be extraordinary – and that's most of us. It's particularly a burden when you are shouldering a fair bit of the housework and caring duties, while trying to keep healthy and have a social life tucked in there somewhere. I'd describe that as living a full life, not 'having it all' by the way. But amid all of those activities, it is dauntingly off-putting to confront the idea that no matter how much you achieve or how efficient you are, the fact that you are female is at some level framing and colouring your actions. I sometimes describe this dynamic as the difference between having the benefit of the doubt – which is usually extended to men, at least initially – and fighting for credibility as a female. It's a grind to be forced to constantly prove your worth and it's exhausting. No wonder women sometimes ask me if maybe it would be best if we all just put our heads down and got on with it and let someone else with fire in their feminist belly do the agitating. Well, no. As tempting as that sounds it just isn't going to lead to change and we know that because these myths have survived and even thrived for that exact reason.

I have deliberated about the main contenders for myth-busting, and there are quite a few more I could have tackled (women lack confidence, for example, or take too long to make decisions). However, many years of writing and speaking about this topic with all kinds of people and in every major city in Australia has given me a pretty clear idea of what is being discussed in this area at an individual and corporate level, as well as the broader social conversation on gender. Luckily this discussion is no longer confined to women and a growing number of men turn up at forums these days, some a little reluctantly perhaps, but they are there nonetheless. No matter how much agitation there is from women, improvements to this scenario also have to be about men, particularly those with the power to make a difference and influence attitudes.

I think some of the inertia until recent times has

come from the misguided belief that we live in a post-feminist world and 'all that stuff' got sorted out, so whatever happens in workplaces now is not about gender but personal choice. The currency of the 7 myths shows this to be far from the truth. Propping up these myths too is an outdated series of workplace practices developed for a male breadwinner model, now well past its use-by date. I'm realistic about challenging these structures and know we can't transform society and the corporate world quickly by just rebutting the myths. But I'm optimistic that we can influence our cohort and have found that a judicious sprinkling of facts and research to defend one's point of view is an important tool when this topic comes up. It's remarkable how the same questions arise in just about any debate relating to gender and jobs, and I have reflected this in my selection.

Obviously there are areas of overlap too, so I have tried to cross-reference my myths as much as possible and in the process realised that belief in the classic meritocracy, or even playing field myth (myth 1), has a lot to answer for, playing a part in just about every myth. I figured it was important to make those connections clear, to accentuate the harm from letting one set of misconceptions fuel another. Many of these themes have been tackled in 'Corporate Woman' and in the pages of the *Financial Review*, so I have incorporated a number of my columns and articles throughout the book, also using some of the case studies that caught my eye at the time or pertinent interviews.

Debunking the myths has also involved taking a closer critical look at some of the current business efforts to address 'diversity' – an unfortunate corporate euphemism that avoids mentioning women or gender (see myth 1). The myths have certainly hampered efforts to research and test the best methods for making progress. There's a willing audience these days for a neat package to tick the diversity box, as many Australian organisations belatedly focus on how to comply with some of the new reporting measures, such as those for ASX companies introduced in 2011 and in the revised Workplace Gender Equity legislation.

For many in business this is uncharted territory and the hunt for a solution is music to the ears of a new breed of diversity consultants, so a wave of programs, workshops and tools – often promising a quick fix – has been doing the rounds. The myths are still colouring many of these efforts, so my advice is to take a 'buyer beware' approach to some of these 'solutions'. We've been hearing about women's mentoring and sponsoring programs, networking groups, diversity training and pay audits, gender targets and even becoming 'gender bilingual', and the topic du jour is unconscious bias. Many of these will be examined a bit more closely in the next chapters to assess if they are helping or hindering the myth-busting.

While I'm not suggesting all these efforts should be ditched, it must be acknowledged that there are some time-wasting diversions around too. On the other hand, I think women do need forums to talk about this topic because it's all too easy to believe the barriers they encounter are all their own fault and they need to learn from others' experiences. Getting men involved in this conversation is a great idea too, as is examining how bias can infiltrate business practices. However, some trends smack of bandwagons. Unconscious bias, for example, appeals to the business world because it is not overtly about gender and thus avoids a more tricky conversation. Understanding how and why the myths evolved and persist raises some of these difficult kinds of questions that are more likely to deliver useful answers. If there's one thing we know now after years of inaction it's that a circuit breaker is needed to avoid more time and effort being wasted in reinforcing the status quo.

That's what the readers of 'Corporate Woman' tell me they are ready for – and they are good enough to get in touch to let me know what they think of the column, both positive and negative. Many say they have cut out the column and pinned it to the tearoom wall, which is highly motivating for me. I suppose it is also evident that a publication like the *Financial Review* attracts a readership skewed to those in professional and white-collar jobs and management, but it certainly reaches a wider range of readers too. Many of those who follow the column have a personal and professional interest in issues such as flexible work, maternity leave and childcare provisions, careers and leadership, as well as the whole gamut of cultural factors that influence social change, philanthropy and small business issues. They may be running an office or their own business or simply trying to hold down a job in a demanding environment, and I am always conscious of the range of information they may be looking for and using in their workplaces.

Given this audience, however, there are areas that are not regularly tackled in the column, but which are, of course, parts of this conversation, such as violence against women, health and reproductive rights, and the problems faced by Indigenous women. Often the focus of the column is on career issues, the professions or the debate around such practical issues as tax deductibility of childcare fees. These are sometimes labelled middle-class welfare concerns that are of less importance than those problems facing low income and casual workers, and women living in developing countries. I think that view needs to be rebutted upfront, mainly because it is a tactic to make women give up and shut up, and it doesn't make sense. After all, if we give up our middle-class fight the result will be middle-class white men retaining the power and status, which is hardly going to lift women out of poverty in the developing world.

This argument and defence of the myths remind us that what we are struggling to access is being firmly defended because it is worth having – it's about power and influence in and beyond workplaces. We need women to aspire to and reach management and leadership positions, because they can then make decisions that affect a range of employees and become role models to those coming up through the ranks. If these women are not at the table then the slow change to our workplaces will grind to a halt. We need them to be there, representing a women's perspective, normalising women's participation and different career trajectories. They are part of the essential effort to legitimise women as leaders in organisations and society, and change the debate.

I've noticed arguments that depend on an either/or dichotomy often crop up when the subject of women and work is discussed. Either you are a good mother or a good worker, a professional on the job or a nice person, grateful for a decent job or a selfish, privileged complainer. The myths have been a handy way of perpetuating this trade-off in roles that hamper all women and help keep alive the notion that women in white-collar jobs are just never satisfied. I think the fact that women with these advantages are finding it difficult to be treated fairly means we have a real problem, not a reason to be ashamed and give up. The principles of gender equity are universal and don't prevent us from mobilising around causes to support those from less advantaged backgrounds and in all parts of the world. Paying women less than men for the same job is a problem whether you live in Sydney or Dhakar, and it is not culturally relative.

This topic came up in when I had the great privilege of interviewing film maker and activist Abigail Disney (granddaughter of Roy Disney) shortly before she visited Australia in 2011. Her documentary, *Pray the Devil Back to Hell* premiered in 2008 and focuses on the peace movement of local women in Liberia, who later helped elect Ellen Johnson-Sirleaf president. Along with Liberian peace activist Leymah Gbowee, Johnson-Sirleaf won the 2011 Nobel Peace Prize. Now the film has been shown as part of a mini-series, *Women, War and Peace*, which premiered in the United States in October 2011, exploring women's roles in conflict in Colombia, Afghanistan, Bosnia and Liberia. Disney made the point that women have transformed philanthropy through their special interest in the 'girl effect', and were needed at the table to make a change happen in relation to the way funds are distributed to those in need.

Women in the US have changed the philanthropic world, not just on women's issues but looking for local participation. That is something that has totally come out of the women's funding movement. I like to avoid saying 'women do this and men do that' but it's important to have at a high level some difference in the way people operate. At a high level women tend to hand out the money to more organisations at greater rates.

While the problems facing women in the developing world were enormous, Disney pointed out that women working for better gender equity in Australian workplaces should never feel that their efforts are trivial or less worthwhile.

To fight for equality and the things women need in the workplace isn't going to prevent us doing the work in other parts of the world. To imply we should drop that is stupid. We went to the Congo and spoke to women and showed them the film and asked them to identify their five top priorities. Not one of those groups of women leaders identified sexual violence as their top three: every single one said women's political empowerment and leadership for women.

I wonder if this sense that our efforts are inconsequential or selfish is another manifestation of the feminist backlash. It's certainly the word that dare not speak its name, particularly in business settings. Yet there is nothing wrong with calling the proud human rights movement for women by its established and historically resonant name – despite successful campaigns to co-opt the word so it is synonymous with man-hating extremism. It's a shame because without feminism we would not even have the myths to bust, because access to paid work would be a pipe dream for most of us. I love the advice from journalist Caitlin Moran, in *How to be a Woman*, to not only use the word but to add 'strident' to the description just to make the point. After railing against the number of women who refuse to be identified as feminists, she has realised that it's technically impossible for a woman to argue this case.

'Without feminism you wouldn't be allowed to have a debate on a woman's place in society. You'd be too busy giving birth on the kitchen floor ... the more women argue, loudly, against feminism, the more they both prove it exists and that they enjoy its hard-won privileges.' She points out that it's not as though the US black activists of the 1960s rejected civil rights as a description of their activism. And the idea that feminism is a punitive kind of club that demands certain standards or condemns you for all eternity is also way off the mark. 'What is feminism? Simply the belief that women should be as free as men however nuts, dim, deluded, badly dressed, fat, receding, lazy and smug they might be.'

Feminism isn't a club, and if it were, membership would be open to everyone, just as all women share in the results of its successful campaigns. The evidence and arguments about the myths actually reveal that the outlook for women employees in Australia remains in the doldrums throughout the economy and the working ranks. Women are still paid less, are far more likely to be in insecure casual work, have far less superannuation, and are still over-represented in lower paid and low-skilled ranks and sectors. And they still do 80 per cent of the housework. Their efforts are judged differently and, unlike the range of behaviour deemed valid for men in the workplace, women are restricted to a much narrower band of acceptable options, which can be confusing and punitive.

Tackling these problems is a classic feminist endeavour that cuts across demographics, and through any concerns about muddying the waters of feminist ideology by advocating that women become replicas of male wage slaves. Germaine Greer once said: 'I didn't fight to get women out from behind vacuum cleaners to get them onto the board of Hoover'. I take her point. After all, why would women want to replicate those traditional power structures? It's not as though the current system works very well for all. However, ensuring most women have a fair chance of financial independence and security is a fundamental right that would never be questioned for men. Access to that is worth the effort.

Despite my close scrutiny of this area over several decades, it does continue to surprise me that many in the business world can profess to be in search of some real answers to gender inequity while remaining completely blasé about the evidence that debunks the myths. I am convinced that now is the time to push the case and tackle them, because, as the ubiquitous diversity programs demonstrate, there's a window of opportunity for some attention which we dare not waste. A few short years ago this was certainly not the case, but a backward slide in women's represen-tation in 2008 shocked even the business world into some recognition that all was not well. The fact that the dangers of quotas and targets qualify at all for inclusion here (myth 5) reflects this shift. Others are old favourites, such as the pipeline (myth 7) – the idea that time will heal all – and the so-called deficit model (myth 6) contending women will be OK if they just act more like men, plus I've also added my own bête noir, that women are their own worst enemies. I have tackled the gender pay gap (myth 2), and women's lack of ambition (myth 3), and tried to tease out the bias that still means many men believe women are simply not ambitious per se because they don't behave like alpha males.

Just like the overlap in the actual myths

themselves, the effective ways of tackling the barriers will be about a range of approaches, as well as different attitudes and behaviour. It is not going to happen quickly or naturally, because this kind of shift never does, but myth-busting can help. The more I research and write about this topic the more I am convinced that the changes to norms and practices discussed here will result in a better way of working for all of us, not just for women. As I say to audiences, this is not a discussion that is anti-men, it is pro-women, and while it can be confusing and confronting, discuss it we must. Then every so often, sometimes when you least expect it, refuting the myths changes someone's mind.

While I call my list 'myths', I do understand that of course there are women who believe females are not ambitious, are innately poor at negotiating, and better off caring for the children and cleaning the kitchen. But apart from the fact that those opinions are generally coloured by the context in which they are made (as I will examine in myth 1), they do not apply to all women, just as male stereotypes don't apply to all men. I have worked with men who were empathetic and great communicators and with women who were not. I also know virtually no women who believe they are innately less capable of doing their job because of their gender, that they deserve lower pay for doing the same work as a man or ultimately that being female is a marker of inferiority. The myths have survived because they are fuelled by these quite fundamental but unspoken beliefs.

Meanwhile, despite some renewed vigour, there is also still much work to be done in putting this topic back on the agenda and legitimising the entire debate in the business sector, instead of tinkering around the edges. It takes real guts to counter the accepted wisdom and speak out, and it can be risky too, as many women (and some male sympathisers) have learnt to their detriment. Whingeing women are universally loathed, and in Australia there's nothing more derided than a bolshie woman. Having our first woman prime minister was hailed as a breakthrough, but it has also proved a somewhat depressing example of how far we have to go to dismantle our traditional notions about women and formal leadership and the double standards the myths help to support. This is still the case despite also having a woman governor-general and attorney general, a female premier and several federal ministers, judges, vice chancellors and the small but outstanding group of women directors, CEOs and senior executives. While their presence is a cause for great optimism, the reaction to them confirms they are regarded as the exception rather than the rule.

Normalising women's participation as leaders, decision-makers and workers in all walks of life has driven me to attack the myths. I hope you find this book useful – it is certainly information-rich. I hope you can pick it up whenever a particular issue grabs your attention, as each chapter is self-contained and contains case studies plus numerous references to research from Australia and internationally. If just one fact or observation sticks in your mind and helps you to puncture part of a myth, my work here will be done and I'll be a happy (strident) feminist.

MYTH 1:
WORKPLACES ARE MERITOCRACIES

The meritocracy defence of workplace dynamics could be first or last on my hit list, because it underpins every one of the other myths in this book. It's embedded in corporate mission statements, chanted by executives and repeated ad nauseam by a lot of people who should know better, or who really should have a long hard think about what they are stating with such certainty. After hearing merit come up in forums just about every time I have been involved in a gender equity discussion, I have come to realise it is a bedrock belief for many of us, male and female. I reckon it's so tenacious because we all want to believe that we work in places and with people who are scrupulously fair in all circumstances. In fact, that's probably particularly true in Australia where egalitarianism is something we pay a lot of lip service to, and could be considered as part of our national psyche. It's no coincidence that 'fair enough' and 'fair go' are part of our vernacular.

However, as I often point out when I hear this term glibly stated during a gender and workplace discussion, meritocracies by definition will not result in a startlingly homogenous group rising magically to the top of the pile. If you accept that talent can come from any part of the population – and history would certainly bear this out – then the people who succeed should represent a broad spectrum of backgrounds, ages, gender and race. But take a look at our major organisations and you will see they are still dominated at the top by white, middle-aged men. Can motherhood really be the only reason that the ASX200 have just 2.5 per cent women chairs, 3 per cent CEOs, 13.5 per cent directors and 8 per cent executive managers, according to the *Australian Census of Women in Leadership*? If that's a meritocracy then it's about a very particular kind of merit that must reside in a narrow cohort of the population, sometimes called the pale, male and stale.

A few years ago I heard the then Deputy Prime Minister Julia Gillard tell a forum on women and work in Sydney that she is a firm believer in the principle that merit is spread throughout the population. In this country it would be reasonable to assume that many of us theoretically agree with this proposition. Great writers, poets, footballers, swimmers, actors and film directors come in all shapes and sizes. When you think about it in that way, clearly talent is not restricted to a particular slice of society or race, religion or gender group. Surely business isn't so different from other domains that its demand for skill and talent can only be met by one group? As a liberal democracy we have seen a broad range of people changing the complexion of our government, education system, shops, neighbourhoods and, yes, parts of the business community. But go beyond a certain level to those in charge and that rapidly turns into homogeneity.

So after thinking about this, I decided that an examination of the myth of meritocracy and the idea we all work on an 'even playing field', would have to be first in the book because it plays such an important part in propping up the thinking that keeps my myths circulating. It's dangerous on a number of levels, as I will examine, but its popularity over recent years as corporate dogma is probably to do with a certain amount of wish fulfilment by those in power. They use the merit myth to convince themselves that they got where they are today because they – and, strangely enough, a lot of people who look just like them – are simply better equipped than anybody else for the top jobs, and that they received no particular favours along the way. So those who failed to get ahead simply have themselves to blame. As with all the myths, it is also a highly subjective assessment, often based on assumptions and fed by stereotypes, and therefore particularly tricky to pin down and challenge. But this much has become clear to me; when it is repeated with authority by those in charge, or enshrined as a 'corporate value', it has an enormously damaging effect literally and metaphorically for those who belong to a group that is conspicuously absent from the top of the 'meritricious' pile.

That doesn't mean it's not a worthwhile goal. When I speak about the meritocracy myth at forums I often quote Mahatma Gandhi's response when he was asked by an English journalist in the 1930s what he thought of western civilisation: 'I think it would be a good idea'. The notion of merit and meritocracies is tenacious, according to Karen Morley, academic and co-founder of Melbourne consulting firm, Gender Worx:

> The idea of merit is held very strongly as a value and a lot of organisations are very keen to be meritocracies. There's a focus on development programs and reinforcing the notion that merit sits under those processes. But it's not the case that everyone gets the same opportunities and chance of promotion.

While she believes that a meritocracy may be the stated objective, it is important to understand the influence of our models of what a leader and leadership look like, and how this is shaped by informal beliefs and attitudes linked to our social and cultural expectations. Women are still not seen as authority figures, are often less visible because of flexible work arrangements, and are more reluctant to put themselves forward for development opportunities due to family constraints. But even if they are in fact keen to pursue a career, the odds against them making the pool of contenders are pretty bad and reflect a lot of covert discrimination which is known as 'second generation' gender bias. These are the largely invisible but potent inhibitors to a true meritocracy, and some large-scale studies in recent years have made this clear.

According to research by not-for-profit US firm Catalyst, men are twice as likely as women to hold a CEO or senior executive position and less likely to be at lower levels, where women are over-represented. Parenthood and level of aspiration do not explain the results, as the findings considered women and men without children, as well as those who aspired to senior leadership positions. Men, in general, were also found to be more satisfied with their careers overall than women. Thus, the report concluded, despite well-intentioned programs, companies around the globe have neglected to develop talented women and failed to build meritocracies.

Even among graduates of elite Master of Business

Administration programs, women continue to lag behind men at every single career stage, right from their first professional jobs. Reports of progress in advancement, compensation and career satisfaction are at best overstated, and at worst just plain wrong, said Catalyst's Nancy Carter and Christine Silva, when the study was released. Well-educated young women generally do not start off on an equal footing with their male peers in the United States, and this is also true in Australia, where Gradstats 2010 data show that female graduates earn $2000 less per year on average than male graduates when they start work. According to Carter and Silva:

> Even after adjusting for years of work experience, industry and region, Catalyst found men started their careers at higher levels than women. And that isn't because women don't aspire to the top – the finding holds when you include only women and men who say they're aiming for senior executive positions. It's not a matter of parenthood slowing women's careers either. Among women and men without children living at home, men still start at higher levels.

With the odds stacked against women at entry level, the faith that growing numbers of women entering the workplace will rectify the problem is way off the mark (see myth 7). With this kind of evidence it is difficult to understand how most organisations can continue to claim they are meritocracies.

Catalyst also highlighted familiar assumptions about demographics and life choices: that women leave to start families (myth 4) and don't aspire to upper management (myth 3), and that regional differences skew results. They concluded, 'These have become handy excuses for gender inequity in the management ranks, even putting the onus on female employees for the discrepancies. But our results suggest they're red herrings that don't account for why women continue to lag'.

The conclusion that women's careers simply don't progress like men's is corroborated by another large 2009 study, *Holding Women Back;* the deck is stacked against women from the earliest days of their careers. The findings revealed that female leaders are under-represented in accelerated development programs early on in their careers, hindering their climb up the ladder.

Because many of the accelerated programs (like high potential programs and one-on-one mentorship) are secret or happen behind closed doors, organizations aren't held accountable for gender balance. Having women represented in significant numbers at every leadership level doesn't mean that will carry to the executive level – in fact, there is a backlash against women at the top when they are dominant in leadership roles at every other level.

While these studies don't exactly lift the spirits, it is helpful to have this kind of thoughtful analysis emerging in recent times, instead of assuming the problems for women are imagined or mostly to do with women's failings. The studies make it clear that assuming merit is the only criteria to get ahead in workplaces is simply not the case, particularly if you are female. They also confirm that the problems with this myth are similar in many developed economies. UK-based consultant Avivah Wittenberg-Cox works with companies around the world and sees the same thinking in many countries. In her blog, 'Corporate leadership is still all about the boys', she said:

> Most male leaders in the companies I work
> with are truly convinced that they work in a
> meritocracy ... Most male managers I work
> with have no idea how male normed today's
> corporate cultures, management mindsets, and
> policy processes still are. Many haven't given it
> a moment's thought. As anyone who has worked
> internationally and cross-culturally knows, you
> have no idea how much you are a product of the

country you come from until you leave it. And most senior male executives have never (yet) left their male-dominated environments and companies. They have rarely experienced the pleasure of being the only man in a roomful of women. When they do, it usually has a profound impact – and they are very often amazed to discover how uncomfortable it can be.

And many women buy into the idea of a male style of merit too, she added.

The result is that many companies only promote women who adopt male styles that can then be recognized as 'talent'. This then creates a negative cycle where younger women are demotivated by the inauthentic, adaptive women held up to them as role models. They quit (physically or intellectually), often citing 'personal reasons,' and then companies complain about a retention problem.

That's the problem with and the reason for the strength of the merit myth. Those who do make it up the ladder are more likely to reproduce and endorse it because the system has worked for them and they have a vested interest in defending rather than analysing the status quo. But I believe it has more to answer for.

When you are sure your cohort is the one that reflects merit you also tend to only trust people who look and talk like you. This why the homogenous cohort at the senior levels of many organisations continues to replicate itself (the ASX200 boards anyone?), while regarding any deviation from the norm as a bit risky. Indeed, as Origin Energy and Macquarie Group chair Kevin McCann told a forum on gender in early 2012, most of the men on the top 50 boards in Australia all went to the same schools, universities, married each other's sisters and go on holidays to the same places.

Margaret Heffernan, author of *Wilful Blindness*, believes it's part of our psychology and a very human tendency to favour feelings of comfort and recognition or intuition over evidence. She says there is also a tendency for the powerful to truly believe that their success is all due to innate brilliance, whereas in fact the roles themselves confer a substantial amount of that clout. When a CEO demands that something is done it usually happens. It doesn't take long for the powerful to believe it is them, not their position, that is having an effect and without some perspective executives can easily fall into the trap of taking all the credit. When they are surrounded mainly by other powerful, white, middle-aged men who believe the same thing, there's a self-perpetuating tendency to think the people with merit and natural prospects for management and the C suite are mostly these exact kinds of alpha blokes. In fact, the existence of any homogenous power group is actually a sign that there probably is no meritocracy in operation. More and more studies are finding that those like-minded and look-alike groups do not reflect a meritocracy and are actually the risky option when it comes to decision making.

So a mix is the better option, and it turns out women can make a positive difference to groups. The best operating teams tend to be those with more women, according to Anita Woolley and Thomas Malone, writing in the *Harvard Business Review*. This is not because women are intellectually or morally superior to men, but they do tend to be more socially sensitive. In fact, there is little correlation between a group's collective intelligence and the IQs of its individual members, according to the researchers. But if a group includes more women its collective intelligence rises.

According to Woolley, 'Many of the factors you might think would be predictive of group performance were not things like group satisfaction, group cohesion, group motivation – none were correlated with collective intelligence. And, of course, individual intelligence wasn't highly correlated, either.' That's right: the sum of the IQ scores did not predict top performance. 'When it comes to the best blend, the standard argument is that diversity is good and you should have both men and women in a group. But the data show that so far the more women the better.' While it is a generalisation to conclude the results are solely due to women being more socially sensitive (after all, some men also have those skills), the findings nevertheless reinforce the message that having a broader range of people with an array of different attributes adds up to a better outcome. The researchers found that a strong operating team seems to be about the dynamic between the members, which is enhanced when a group is diverse in areas such as gender and age and in views as well. Agreement isn't just an inhibitor to better outcomes, it's a danger. In fact, the more bonhomie in a team, the higher the chance of group-think.

'The downside of the cosy feeling of togetherness is that everyone is less vigilant and more vulnerable to bad and dangerous decisions,' according to Margaret Heffernan. But there are other dangers from a cosy homogenous team: because they become so sure of the superiority of their perspective they are more prone to demonise outsiders or dissenters. 'In most organisations the good team player is implicitly defined as the person who goes along with the team, not the one who asks hard questions. In fact, of course, being a truly good team player involves having the confidence to dissent.'

A few years ago, as the Halifax Bank of Scotland

(HBOS) was teetering on the brink of collapse, Heffernan was running a panel discussion about board governance in London that included the HBOS chair, Dennis Stevenson. Not only did he show up for the panel, which surprised many, given the chaos, but he then waxed lyrical about the unanimity of the board in the face of the crisis. The concept that this very unity may have been one of the causes of the problem did not seem to have occurred to Stevenson, according to Heffernan.

Not so long ago I heard a well-known Australian business figure and director asked about the low level of women on boards at a panel discussion. He defended the status quo by earnestly explaining that the most important quality for a smoothly operating board was for all the directors to feel comfortable. Needless to say, by implication, more women directors represented less comfort for him. This was not well received by the audience of superannuation fund managers he was addressing, who were critical of the stock market performance of their substantial investment in many listed companies, and keen to see better performing boards. It's safe to say the women directors sitting on the panel with the comfortable man were not impressed either.

The ingredients of a high-performing group – which sounds more like the result of a genuine meritocracy at work – is about the sum of the parts, as found by the *Harvard Business Review* research. Great groups are not those where the members are all really smart, according to Woolley, but where the members listen to each other. 'They share criticism constructively. They have open minds. They're not autocratic. And in our study we saw pretty clearly that groups that had smart people dominating the conversation were not very intelligent groups.' So picking a team of colleagues who look and think like you may be standard business practice, but it is usually not going to reflect those with the most merit, will not generate the best results and could well be dangerous.

Nevertheless, our meritocracy myth lives on. As well as being inaccurate and reinforcing the cookie cutter approach to appointing top teams, this label provides the perfect excuse to maintain the status quo. I have been repeatedly told by senior male executives over many years that they firmly believe everyone in the organisation has had the same opportunities as them, and so they conclude there can't be anything wrong with the system – it must be the individuals. Cream rises to the top, they tell themselves. No wonder they are not motivated to examine the way the system works or look at the behaviour of those making important decisions. According to Catalyst research by Prime and colleagues in 2009, 'Before individuals can support a change initiative, they must first be convinced that there is something wrong with the status quo ...'

As long as there's adherence to the idea that merit really does sort out the men from the boys (pun intended), there will be deep-seated scepticism about the existence of a gender equity problem. The attitudes towards some of the diversity activity in recent years may be theoretically endorsed by the CEO and the top team, but some Australian research suggests that if you scratch the surface a very different view emerges that helps the myth live on. One study of the Australian financial services sector by the Financial Services Institute in 2010 revealed a rather basic disagreement between men and women about the nature of gender disparities and, indeed, the validity of such issues.

The majority of respondents (64 per cent men) said they had never observed or directly experienced different treatment of females in promotions, meetings, training opportunities, pay or inclusion in social activities. This alleged blindness to what is going on under their noses is, unfortunately, not unusual. So far, so predictable. But the results get really interesting when split by gender. There's a huge difference in opinion about the existence of the well-documented barriers women continue to face at work. While 71 per cent of the men surveyed believe that companies have taken significant steps to address the structural disadvantages, so that women now have the same opportunities as men, 72 per cent of women disagreed. There was a similar disparity in the attitudes to a gender pay gap.

The same kind of perception gap was picked up in management consultancy McKinsey & Company's 2010 global survey of 1500 executives, from middle management to CEOs across multiple sectors, on this issue. The study claimed that companies with the highest share of women on their executive committees financially outperform those with all-male executive committees, and while not demonstrating causality, this provides a strong factual basis for arguing the case for more women in top management. Yet, only 62 per cent of male executives were convinced of the positive impact of diversity on performance, compared with 90 per cent of women. The gap was even bigger at middle management level (50 per cent of men, 85 per cent of women). McKinsey also identified a knowing and doing gap. In spite of the performance data, only 28 per cent of companies had put gender among their top ten priorities, and 32 per cent had no specific measures.

When this denial about bias goes underground, accompanied by a belief in the even playing field, it's even harder to identify and address. There's still overt and covert belief in the meritocracy mantra. I heard that a group of middle managers at a financial services firm even organised themselves into an 'anti-diversity club' and went away on weekends for some 'male bonding' time to register their resentment at efforts in this area. More often there's grumbling about – you guessed it – unfairness. 'You have to be a woman to get ahead these days' is the common complaint from disgruntled men, who seemingly had no problem with the fact that you've had to be male to get ahead for the last few millennia or so. The myth plays a role in perpetuating this unhelpful discourse too. There has always been whingeing about special programs or paid maternity leave from blokes who see any moves to assist women as unfair because they tell themselves the workplace offers everyone the same opportunities and women are getting a special advantage.

The meritocracy myth has also continued to hamper women's representation on boards (see myth 5). Dianne Rodgers-Healey, from the Australian Centre for Leadership for Women, compiled a study called *Women Getting into Boards*, on board appointments. Most respondents were women and many held directorships. Her results revealed that the recruitment process of boards is predominantly inequitable as it lacks transparency and clearly defined and realistic criteria. Positions are advertised to a select group and women usually have less opportunity to apply because they do not know where there are vacancies or what the requirements are for the job. The research particularly took issue with the often-repeated idea that somehow women with enough 'merit' automatically make it onto a shortlist. Rodgers-Healey said:

I challenge and debate the whole idea of merit appointments – women are never given the chance to develop merit. It's a very elitist idea. How can you get to merit when you are not in the door? All the way through your career you are disadvantaged and can't get that merit that will make you on an equal par as a man.

The problems women face are more complex, and even those who get to the stage of identifying and applying for a board role may run up against indirect barriers. 'When they do apply, they are judged against criteria which are discriminatory and attitudes which rate their achievements and experiences as unimportant and un-transferable.'

Insidious and persistent as the concept of merit can be, there is some good news; bald statements that 'our business is a meritocracy' are finally starting to wear thin. The gap between rhetoric and reality is turning into a chasm that is so wide it's getting hard to ignore, particularly with today's employees, who are much more savvy about organisational spin. There are welcome signs that this myth may be up for some more scrutiny as the debate on gender in business gathers pace in Australia, as it has in other countries. It's encouraging to hear some CEOs admit they relied on their belief in a meritocracy when considering gender gaps in their organisations, but have since realised there was much more to the problem than this rather passive platitude.

Most saw the light after some myth-busting by people they respect. So far the penny dropping hasn't exactly led to revolutionary change, but some executives acknowledge it's time for a rethink. I heard Gail Kelly, CEO of Westpac, admit that the lack of gender equity progress in recent years at the bank was probably because there was a belief the work had already been done to ensure a fairer workplace and attention had moved on. Realising this was not the case, pressure needed to be re-applied, she said. Several of the members of the Male Champions of Change group, a lobby group made up of some of Australia's top CEOs, acknowledge that a meritocracy is an aim rather than necessarily a reality throughout their organisations.

As I already mentioned, the impact of this belated awareness, along with the need to comply with the self-regulatory regimes introduced, has seen a rash of 'diversity' initiatives launched since 2010 in the business world, including mentoring programs, targets for women in senior jobs, diversity policies and corporate governance reporting changes. Some companies have recorded encouraging results, having removed some biased processes and finding that merit was not the sole criteria for recruitment or promotion. But there is still some way to go and as a seasoned observer of this arena I think there will be some failures too.

Often programs aimed at assisting women can reinforce the idea that they lack the ever more confusing ingredients for merit. This is because many are still based on the remedial approach to changing gender representation that concentrates on and emphasises women's lack of appropriate skills and inability to behave like assertive men, while clinging to the belief that a set of objective standards for merit exists (myth 5). As the Catalyst research suggests, there are some very different reasons why women struggle to climb the ladder or get paid equitably. The lack of anything resembling a meritocracy, and old-fashioned bias towards the existing power group in most organisations is, in fact, one of the key reasons so few women make it into senior jobs.

The existence of the ubiquitous diversity council and diversity manager in organisations is often a sign that little is actually happening to seriously address systemic gender imbalances masked by the meritocracy idea, according to Avivah Wittenberg-Cox. She is no fan of the word 'diversity' because it lumps separate issues under a label palatable to management.

> I don't think gender should be part of diversity, I think framing it as part of diversity is why it hasn't worked. It's better pulling it out [of the diversity area]. Most managers would much prefer to do anything but gender. They don't

want to call it gender so they call it diversity because it is more acceptable. The two issues that carry across borders are gender and [workplace] culture. You can't do race [discrimination] in the same way, it has to be national.

The senior business teams that Wittenberg-Cox works with usually have blind spots when it comes to gender bias:

> Most are convinced they work in a meritocracy and make assumptions about what's going on. And many companies are well intentioned and put in policies and benchmarking to fix the women, networks and coaching and mentoring, and it hasn't delivered anything. And they are frustrated that hasn't worked. I do a lot of work in professional services firms and they think their business model is the only way they can function, in an aggressive alpha male profile, and they think women just can't do it.

The tipping point comes, she said, when only people who know how to manage in this area will be promoted and gender inclusion efforts are made an attractive management competency – without which your career will be compromised.

Some of the educational effort to identify the

pitfalls of relying on a mythical notion of merit would also be helped along by a clearer analysis of all the human resources talk about self-managed careers, personal branding and 'Me Inc' (an expression coined by management guru Tom Peters). As a management writer, I've seen increasing emphasis on individualism infiltrate organisational thinking. In the corporate world, the old days of training and developing all employees within the business are long gone. This has driven a demand for more and more professional employees to use external coaches and mentors to get ahead these days (sometimes at their own expense). It's a move away from the mid-twentieth-century idea of 'organisation man' (and they were all men) with a job for life, trained and supported by a paternal employer and heavily influenced by the workplace and its standards.

The rhetoric has swung over to suggest individual employees all have discretion over their careers, with much less attention paid to the power of the hierarchy, the management, the corporation and, indeed, social standards. This shift has helped the meritocracy myth along by reinforcing the idea that you reap what you alone sow, and there is little impact on your progress from context, subjectivity in performance assessment and promotion, and behavioural norms in the workplace. Many women find out the hard way that despite being told a strong work ethic will generate its own rewards, regardless of anything else, the reality is quite different.

For all the talk about diversity programs there's also a whole range of ways in which merit is not being enabled in many daily business practices, according to Gender Worx consultant Karen Morley, and analysing recruitment or promotion procedures and 'value' statements would help. It's also pivotal for companies wanting to see results to talk about the gender issue as something for which men and women both have responsibility. This can change the way we tackle it, and men have a much greater impact if they role-model ways to behave in a gender-neutral way. Understanding how women fit into the organisation and how they also need to negotiate their careers is important because women have biases, too. 'Women need to accept women as authority figures and project that as well.'

Some of the awareness-raising about merit remains superficial and there is no reason to assume this myth will simply disappear in coming years. As pressure to report on gender representation in business mounts and other measures come into practice, with some poor results revealed, there's bound to be some continued reliance on the merit excuse in the future. Quite a few business leaders, for example, have objected to the concept of quotas or even voluntary targets for women (myth 5) on boards and in senior management on the basis that their organisations are already meritocracies.

As I have highlighted in my column, if a true meritocracy means that senior ranks reflect the talents of the entire workforce then surely targets and quotas for women help rather than hinder this aim? Ensuring that nearly half the workforce is genuinely taken into account for training and development, career planning and promotions ensures the creation of a real meritocracy. There is nothing inherently contradictory about a true meritocracy and quotas or targets, despite the negative commentary they often evoke. They can assist in redressing this imbalance and are not designed to last forever, but to act as a catalyst that can be discarded once the dynamics and composition of boards or senior ranks is changed.

Given the many elements to tackle when dismantling this myth, it's tempting to think that a genuine meritocracy in a competitive business environment is a pipe dream and survival of the fittest will always make it difficult for some talented people to succeed as easily as others. Unpicking this myth is a bit like attacking the house built of cards, where pulling one out can bring the whole lot tumbling down. Once there is some acknowledgement that a whole range of systemic factors favour one cohort over another in the workplace, there's some harsh reality to face about the actual credentials needed to get ahead.

That can be a pretty uncomfortable exercise.

But it's a relatively simple and important step to just stop using the description as a statement of fact and put it where it belongs: as a worthwhile aspiration. I believe the solid research and academic literature on this topic confirms that this is a goal most businesses are still far from reaching. As a result, they are missing out on a wealth of talent and experience at a time in Australia when there is increasing demand for skilled workers.

Next time you hear the word meritocracy, remember to listen carefully. Do you think your workplace is really an even playing field? Working out why this is not so and what to do to change it may involve some interim pain but has enormous benefits for women, for men and for organisations of all kinds.

CASE STUDY: THE PUBLIC SECTOR

In 2010 I wrote about a series of programs that transformed the public sector for women. People such as the CEO of Carnival Australia, Ann Sherry; CEO of Korn Ferry, Katie Lahey; former Sydney Water boss Kerry Schott; former Victorian Police commissioner Christine Nixon; former Esanda chief and board director Elizabeth Proust, all gained crucial experience and opportunities during a massive shake-up in the public sector in the

1980s and 1990s, which was designed to radically alter its culture.

The public service of the 1980s – just like plenty of business sectors today – had women disproportionately clustered in lower-level jobs, paid less than their male peers, and lacking in opportunities for advancement. Women were routinely left off lists for promotion and, until the 1960s, had to resign when they got married. In fact, the private sector could learn a lot from the methods used to change this, according to corporate adviser Jane Bridge, who worked on the New South Wales government's affirmative action program, and is now managing director of advisory firm Boardroom Partners. There was a massive cultural change brought about by the introduction of merit: 'Merit was defined, and that was quite interesting. We asked, 'What is it and how do you assess it?'

Selection committees had to look different. It was all part of a real cultural change that blew open the closed shop. In the 1990s, for example, Victorian premier Joan Kirner moved to include at least one woman on interview panels, which had a marked effect, according to Wendy Simpson, a former Victorian ministerial adviser and now executive chair of Westray Engineering. Once women were on the interviewing panels they were seeing the credentials of people being appointed to senior jobs and looking at their own resumés and understanding how they could put themselves forward. Kirner also made it clear that the industry delegations eager to lobby her had to have at least one senior woman on their team or they would not get through the door. Organisations were forced to find women. And once they took a closer look at their constituency, they did.

A number of women now in senior executive corporate positions and in the professions were officially dubbed 'change agents' in the various state and federal affirmative action programs, according to governance adviser and director Elizabeth Johnstone, a former partner at law firm Blake Dawson. Johnstone herself was a change agent, working with a number of state government bodies, including the New South Wales Audit Office, Fire Brigade and Police Force. Change agents and champions within organisations provided crucial stepping stones to the successful implementation of such programs. Far from being an exercise in political correctness driven by do-gooders, the programs were very clear, objective and data-driven. In every organisation there was a change agent who reported to the CEO to look at policies and processes and to examine the systemic areas of discrimination.

The programs being introduced were often strenuously resisted. Johnstone recalls, 'There were lots of problems and we faced a lot of hostility. We didn't set out to change attitudes, but to change behaviour – and we did change behaviour, gradually.'

The basic principles from the NSW affirmative action

program were later used by networking group Chief Executive Women (CEW) to develop a gender package, The CEO Kit, to help companies improve retention of female talent. CEW used the kit for a number of years to discuss the issues at a senior level and – using their own data – work through approaches to attract and retain women. Jane Bridge, who helped compile the kit, reflected: 'It was all about a data-driven approach: get the data, see what's happening and tailor it to suit your organisations and hit the hot spots first'.

It may be transferrable, but the data needed to help organisations change are not always easy to collect or access, even in large companies. CEW discovered that many organisations keep little information on why women leave. There are plenty of myths, such as 'they leave for family reasons', but few facts to support this, and little other information as to the real reasons behind their decision to leave.

Tips from the public sector experience:

- Comprehensive review of employee utilisation and personnel practices
- Collection of relevant statistical data
- Sophisticated use of questionnaires, interviews and written submissions about particular policies and practices within each organisation
- Training of the change agents themselves

- Publication of the results in a management plan for each organisation
- Ensuring a critical mass when appointing women to senior roles
- The annual public reporting of progress.

MYTH ②:
THE GENDER PAY GAP
IS EXAGGERATED

In early 2012 a watershed decision on gender pay
equity was made to support a pay rise to about
150 000 of Australia's lowest paid workers in the
community services sector – mostly women. It was a
breakthrough because Fair Work Australia had found
that gender did indeed play a role in the undervaluing
of the jobs in this traditional 'caring' sector: childcare
workers, aged care workers. The decision was greeted
with elation in some quarters, particularly those who
had worked long and hard to get the case heard, but
there were grim forecasts and warnings from others.
The critics warned that such pay increases would
cause havoc and lead to job cuts in the sector or even
hurt 'working women' – but not men – by increasing
childcare fees.

The mixed reaction was to be expected, but the
vehemence of the objections and predictions of cost
escalations and childcare shortages did seem extreme.
Caring work is still seen as women's work and such

an association comes with a value judgement, as we will see. However, some of the commentary, implying these workers were greedy and would hurt other women, managed to surprise me, even after many years of watching the debate. The level of resistance and sometimes downright aggression that arises when the gender pay gap is raised is astounding. Of course, there are many areas of the broader debate about discrimination that unleash strong emotions and passionate argument. But this particular area can spark real fireworks – from men and women.

Critics not only take issue with the level of the gender pay gap, which in 2012 is about 17.2 per cent in raw average earnings, but many actually deny there is any proof that the differential has anything at all to do with discrimination. I guess deep down these are the people who also believe a true meritocracy exists in all workplaces, and what we do or don't get in the cut and thrust of work is up to us. But gender pay gap statistics are fairly stark, statistically robust and well documented. Sceptics insist that the pay differential between men and women for similar work is the result of structural and economic differences between male and female labour, of part-time and full-time jobs, of sector differences. And that is true to an extent. But anyone who has expertise in the area can tell you that after taking account of a whole range of these factors there is still up to 60 per cent of the average differential in pay rates between men and women doing the same or similar job for the same number of hours that is unexplained – except by gender discrimination.

Not surprisingly, this goes down like a lead balloon in many business circles. Resistance to the notion that any employer or organisation could have different pay levels based on gender is affronting to many of the people I have discussed this with over the years. And that includes women. After a speech I gave one evening to a group of lawyers a woman approached me and angrily disputed the existence of any such phenomena, swearing she was paid the same as her male peers. Another woman, also a lawyer, joined in the conversation and asked how she knew this was so. After all, there were many pay discrepancies found in bonuses or other forms of variable pay rather than fixed remuneration, which is often based on a scale. A little begrudgingly, the woman who had resisted the notion agreed she was not sure about such bonus levels, which were kept strictly confidential, and conceded it was possible there were variations.

At another forum for women in the oil and gas sector I was fascinated to hear the head of Shell Australia, Ann Pickard, explain that a gender pay gap was discovered among her senior team. When it was investigated the difference was detected not in bonus pay but in fixed salary levels, which for historical reasons were lower for the women involved, despite their seniority.

There are clearly many reasons for the pay gap – all of the myths tackled in this book are contributors to how women's work is valued and assessed in formal workplaces. And, of course, our invisible work as carers and homemakers is attributed to love and not really factored in or valued highly in monetary or other terms.

There are some overarching reasons for the gap too. There is a particularly high degree of occupational segregation in Australia, with nearly 50 per cent of women employees working in just three sectors – health care/ social assistance, education and retail. When that happens these sectors become feminised, which can influence pay scales, as the community services case shows. At more senior levels in business, when it comes to those elusive factors that make a manager decide to increase one person's salary over another of similar ability and experience, the possible array of potential influences and factors is complex. The story is far more complicated than the average pay gap figure suggests and you need to drill into the data, according to Dr Alan Duncan, director of the National Centre for Social and Economic Modelling (NATSEM).

Wage gaps can be explained by different work-related characteristics, different occupational choices, labour market patterns and histories between genders. There are also factors of choice – either guided or forced choice – that exist. Women perhaps disproportionately select employment with lower financial returns and, while this may be a behavioural choice, it is fascinating to consider that behaviour may in fact be conditioned by gender norms and attitudes.

Logically, the differences between the wages of men and women can be partly due to different characteristics or attributes, alongside other aspects, such as selection or choices in occupation, industries and job types. Vocational qualifications, firm size, labour force history differences in terms of time in paid work, tenure of current occupation, and segregation into gender-specific industries, hold some explanatory power. But the overarching finding is that the majority of the wage differential is down to whether you are a woman or a man. If this data is taken a step further, to create equal or equivalent characteristics and job-related attributes between men and women, the study found that about one-third of the pay differential could be explained. Therefore, the stark and overwhelming statistic that lingers is that for the remaining 60 per cent or more that is unexplained, there is no logical reason for the wage differential, Duncan concluded.

What has also become apparent is that the pay gap is not confined to sectors generally described as traditional male employers, such as mining or heavy industry. Financial services organisations are particular laggards when it comes to gender pay differences and getting more women through the ranks, despite employing a workforce that is more than 50 per cent female. So the findings of *Bridging the Gender Divide*, a large study into the sector's management views about this issue, were interesting reading. The respondents, 800 FINSIA members, drawn mostly from middle to executive management, were mainly men (64 per cent), and many worked in retail/commercial banking or financial advice.

Despite years of published data about the gender pay gap and the dwindling number of women in senior roles, there is an extraordinarily high level of denial among this cohort about the problems and causes of women's poor representation. Many male respondents (61 per cent) agreed that 'the pay gap in financial services is grossly exaggerated. The gender difference in earnings is a fair reflection of the hours worked and skill sets.' And 80 per cent of women disagreed. The industry has run out of convenient excuses – a lack of mentoring or networking, for example – to explain the lack of women at the top, according to Martin Fahy, then chief executive of FINSIA. The only way to explain it is to point to a common bias at executive management level towards men and this reflects either a significant perception gap or just plain old complacency, with little desire to enforce gender equality, both in principle and practice.

This kind of thinking is sadly out of step with modern social trends and labour market realities. And it is ironic that a sector that employs the highly numerate and deals with financial data and money-making should be so quick to reject the existence of unfairness in pay levels. But more than anything else, the wide dichotomy in opinions of men and women in this sector speaks volumes about the comfortably unchallenged, stereotypical views of management to this issue, despite years of solid evidence of systemic problems. Given some of the opinions expressed by the senior men, it's not surprising that many financial services firms struggle to attract women to profes-sional jobs or in management ranks.

As a seasoned observer of the pay gap debate, I was nevertheless surprised to learn that the pay gap widens as you go further up the ladder. Research con-ducted by academics Ian Watson, in 2010, and Hiau Joo Kee, in 2006, looked at unexplained gender wage differences. Both their findings concur with the pat-tern that the more senior the position held by a female, the higher the gap in wage patterns. Watson discov-ered that female managers in full-time employment earn 27 per cent less than their male counterparts and that between 65 to 90 per cent of this differential can't be explained by job-related characteristics. He also reported on the evidence of a plateau in labour market experience and suggested that the ongoing existence of the glass ceiling was preventing progression from middle to senior management for females compared with males.

Overall, Watson's analysis found there was a gender difference of $18,500 in remuneration. He looked at how this wage difference could be closed if female characteristics were conferred upon men, including labour market experience, hours worked and equalising the returns to different family characteristics. In fact, it only constituted a fraction of the difference. The most important element in equalising the differential was for a woman to become a man, which would contribute around a $12,500 difference in wages for females. Kee's work reiterated the pattern that wage gaps for lower-paid workers could be explained by job-related characteristics. However, the greatest unexplained gap occurred as one moved up the earnings distribution from the 75th to the 95th percentile, with the greatest difference in the private rather than the public sector.

Not only do women earn less as senior executives, but, according to UK academic Alex Haslam, as CEOs their presence can actually depress the value of the company. Female chief executives also earn much smaller bonuses than men when a company performs well, with an astonishing difference of more than 50 per cent in some cases.

The research, recounted in 'Who gets the carrot and who gets the stick?', involved studying 192 female and male executives in the top 100 listed UK companies from 1998 to 2004. The first thing they discovered was the bonus difference. If you take the worst-performing companies the men are getting bonuses of about £18,000 a year, while the top companies are giving bonuses of about £110,000. For women, the worst-performing got £32,000 and best-performing £36,000.

> It's a flat line for women. The reasons are that when the company has done very well, it [is thought it] must be because it's great leadership – but if a woman is in charge they are looking for other reasons. Men can expect and negotiate for big bonuses, and women are less likely to do that. When men succeed, they think 'I did this and I need credit'. Women are less likely to say 'this was me'.

It was Haslam, along with his colleagues Michelle Ryan and Clara Kulich at the University of Exeter, who conducted the original 'glass cliff' research. The term was coined to describe a pattern in the nature and tenure of women CEO appointments at many of Britain's top-listed companies, following exhaustive research. More often than not, the study found, women come into the CEO role at a time of crisis, and their tenure, by default, is shorter. Women CEOs, the academics went on to discover, are given riskier opportunities, fewer rewards, a sceptical reception and seen as a sign of decline. They are also more likely to be blamed for poor outcomes over which they have little control.

The glass cliff theory got an airing when Julia Gillard became prime minister. Haslam agreed there were some grounds there in which to apply the theory: 'There's talk about Gillard needing to clear up the mess – that's certainly the way people construe the leadership, that's how people see her leadership.' The glass cliff also helps to explain why the small cohort of women corporate leaders earn much less than their male peers. But it gets worse. In a related study the same academics discovered that an adverse sharemarket reaction to women joining a board results in a 38 per cent overvaluation of all-male boards. Haslam noted:

This is not trivial – the size of these phenomena is staggering, really. In other words, companies with all-male boards have a valuation premium of 38 per cent, they are massive numbers. The

GFC [global financial crisis] in the UK was almost entirely due to companies with all-male boards being overvalued. If you want a chronically overvalued company then have an all-male board, but if you are an investor, you want to invest in companies with women on the board because that is a better investment. Those other companies you avoid like the plague.

Far from being exaggerated, he added, the gender differences in remuneration and company valuations are, in fact, statistically robust, but often fobbed off by executives. 'It's the psychology of it. What's one person's gross exaggeration is a statement of the facts to another.'

Perhaps to prove this point, despite the significance of the data on overvaluation the research didn't get much media coverage in the United Kingdom. Critics have also claimed that objective data on company performance does not show any differences regardless of whether there is a woman or a man at the helm. However, Haslam points out that women's presence on the board is associated with subjective underperformance.

There's a paper that came out in the UK, and it shows there's not a difference in objective data. That's correct. It isn't a difference between book value of the company and women's appointment, but there's one in the more subjective measures such as the stockmarket. It seems to be that the stockmarket takes the appointment of a woman as a signal the organisation is in some kind of crisis, and devalues the stock.

Just like those who reject the idea of any significant gender pay gap, there have been plenty of glass cliff deniers, including among women CEOs, but Haslam said the correlation is still valid. There's a gender effect on tenure too, with the average for a male CEO of 8.2 years and 4.8 years for a woman.

One of the things we say is women are in these precarious positions and their tenure shortens. Boards push them out and these jobs are so stressful they move on. One women said to us when she was first interviewed about the glass cliff, 'this is rubbish'. Now she says 'I was in denial'.

Haslam went on to say that it's one thing to produce statistical evidence of bias in these areas, but quite another to convince those in charge to accept and act on it. Deeply held beliefs are hard to shift, particularly when expressed by a powerful CEO. 'The data is very clear. This last paper is putting 600 company years up against the opinion of one CEO. It can be incredibly frustrating. But it is dismantling people's prejudice and it illustrates the points beautifully.'

The work done by Haslam and his colleagues on gender differences in pay, bonuses, and market valuations puts the focus on a core part of the pay gap puzzle. It's about the value we place on women's labour, whether it is individual effort or the effect by association of having a woman leader. Without even knowing it, the structures we work in place a markedly different emphasis and value on certain skills that are associated more with one gender than the other. This is why work is now being done to encourage corporates to not only look closely at pay levels but at job valuation. It's something I've written about several times in the column.

In fact, in 2010 the gap between pay for men and women had widened – reaching 18 per cent based on average weekly earnings. This is roughly the same gap as 25 years ago. Given this evidence there is increasing pressure now on organisations to take some serious steps in addressing the gap, because it's clear it will not resolve itself. While a number of businesses already conduct pay audits, there is plenty more to be done, both within organisations and through stronger external guidelines and tightening up of our self-regulatory framework.

The Equal Opportunity for Women in the Workplace Agency (EOWA) conducted some research in

2010 on the organisations that report to them (which includes a wide range of Australian businesses) to find out if they had undertaken a pay equity analysis. Only about 40 per cent said they had. EOWA found, for example, that few organisations have a history of establishing standards around gender fairness in their formal tools for job assessment. Job evaluation, for example, is the process of ranking the nature, components and types of jobs in an organisation and is used more widely in the United Kingdom. It is important in developing approaches that don't discriminate on the grounds of gender – and can help prevent pay inequity from developing.

My feeling is that the push to address pay gap problems is gathering pace in a number of companies that have managed to overcome the covert scepticism, but the process of pay auditing is complex and needs to be doggedly pursued. Whenever I hear of a successful pay gap resolution it is either after a well-run audit process has identified and then rectified the problem, or an individual has taken her concern and a documented case to her manager. Having the information to identify the problem and then tackle it can work on both levels.

There are factors from outside the workplace that can have a significant impact on women's pay too. The cost of childcare and career breaks both have a massive effect on women's incomes (although childcare costs are, of course, technically a family expense). Sometimes it simply doesn't seem worth the battle to stick with paid work when the costs and hassles of looking after children are factored in – and that continues well beyond the preschool years. It's a complex topic and probably worthy of its own book, but some elements are worth noting here.

There is a renewed push for tax deductibility of childcare costs, which gathered pace again in 2011. Although as Marie Coleman from the National Foundation of Australian Women pointed out to me, the top marginal tax rate of 45 per cent means that tax deductions would only benefit those on high incomes. This is because the current rebate pays 50 per cent of childcare costs, which is not means tested, but capped at $7,500 a year (this does not apply to the cost of an in-home carer). Even having just two children in childcare under the current regime can mean that a substantial proportion of after-tax income goes in fees. A poll conducted in 2012 by consultancy firm The Heat Group found that 52 per cent of Australian women reported childcare as the main barrier to them returning to work after having a child. If you are already paid less because of the gender gap or you are in part-time work the sums often just don't add up.

Given the pressure women feel to justify childcare costs from their salaries (and not the total family income) and the amount involved, it's not hard to see why the gender pay gap becomes even more worrying, and not just because of the impact on women in jobs, but on their future, particularly with an ageing population. The Fair Work conclusion, that there is a gender pay gap for private sector community services employees, has longer-term benefits for the 87 per cent of these workers who are women. There has to be a greater incentive to pursue a career in the sector when there is both an improvement in what you take home now and what you will have to live on in your retirement.

One of the reasons women end up in such poor financial condition near retirement, and then have to rely on the government pension, is that their work record has been broken or they have ended up in casual roles or they are employed in sectors with low pay, making it difficult to put aside super contributions. This is a legacy of a wide range of factors: women's relatively recent entry into education and paid work, while continuing to shoulder the bulk of unpaid domestic labour, and the lingering notion that women will be 'looked after' or that their incomes are secondary to the main breadwinner. I don't think we do our young women any favours when we continue to allow these assumptions to infiltrate all kinds of important decisions, such as whether they should finish school, go on to higher education, and what skills they need for jobs. It's not good enough to tell girls leaving school that it doesn't matter what they do or to find 'something they love'. They have to earn a decent living to look after themselves too.

For all these reasons, Australian women still lag well behind men in accumulating superannuation savings. Women have only 60 per cent of the personal savings of men – on average just $79,100, while men have $132,200 – and alarmingly, women only have half the superannuation of their male counterparts in all age groups from age 35 onwards, according to research carried out by NATSEM and AMP in 2009. The gap has narrowed over the past 20 years, but there is much more to be done as a man still has the potential to earn $2.4 million over a lifetime compared to a woman who earns nearly $1 million less. Nevertheless, awareness among women of the importance of financial security is growing, and just in time because a whole cohort of baby boomer women is approaching retirement and finding their future is looking decidedly precarious. And they know it.

It was cheering to read that women over 50 are not wasting sleep worrying about wrinkles, according to research by blogger Barbara Hannah Grufferman in 2011. Conventional wisdom might say that women of this age are obsessed with holding back the years, and there's big business in convincing us that these should be our focal points, she said.

Women often feel invisible once they are over 50 but that isn't a gut-wrenching fear. It's an observation that most women I know shrug off with a knowing smile. When I asked them to share their worst fear, none of these issues came up. It's clear that these women who are out there working, taking care of their families and contributing to their communities have something much bigger than crow's feet on their minds.

Turns out the one common thread was the fear of not having enough money as they get older.

This didn't exactly shock me as I know many women who deeply rue their decision to leave the workforce, and not just on financial grounds either. But many have ended up with no funds for retirement and few options to earn a decent living. It's a part of the pay gap discussion that is largely ignored, but horribly unfair. As a friend of mine says, these are women who spent their entire lives trying to do what was deemed to be the right thing – looking after the family and home, putting their own needs last, supporting their partner's career and abandoning their job after calculating all the costs of staying in the workforce. These are the some of the long-term repercussions of a lifetime of hard but unpaid work.

Even with all the information we have to hand, refuting the idea that there is no gap and the growing avenues for those wanting to analyse and address it, there's another scapegoat when it comes to women and pay: it's the old belief that actually women would do fine on the pay scale if they could just negotiate properly. All they have to do is sharpen up and behave like men (hmmm, see myth 6) and the pay gap would disappear. Or so it is believed by some of the great and the good. I've been covering this for a long time because it is such a pervasive idea and absorbed by women as well as men. It has never made sense to me because it is stated in such a bald way, as though women are generically incapable of negotiating and it is assumed they get the same encouragement and reception to requests for a pay rise.

Negotiating skills are part of the recipe for success in most management books and often pop up in lists of advice for women wanting to get ahead. According to this line of argument, the only reason women aren't being promoted or getting pay rises like their male colleagues is because they are not asking for either, or they are not asking properly.

This certainly deflects concern away from the structure or norms of workplace systems and onto women's behaviour. That said, there is some evidence that women are more reluctant to put their hands up for more. But to presume that the very real problems of glass ceilings and pay gaps come down to a lack of female negotiating skills, is dangerously simplistic and reinforces inertia and stereotyping around this problem. Outside the workplace women show no particular lack of negotiating skills. Shoe sale anyone? Screaming toddler in supermarket? No worries. In some domains, they are considered the masters of such techniques. This is particularly so when you consider the negotiation required in caring for a home and its inhabitants. Don't start me.

Could it be that most women have no inherent problems with negotiating, but find there is something about workplaces that inhibits the use of those skills? Strangely enough, the fact that there is no such thing as a 'level playing field' in most complex organisations may be well understood by many women, but tell them they are hopeless at something long and loud enough and they will start to believe it. That's why some awareness-raising on what may be contributing to this reluctance to negotiate can help women address the issue and remove some of the taboo from the process. Leslie Alderman, an executive consultant at Chandler Macleod who specialises in coaching executives, told me she has noticed women are particularly reluctant to negotiate, but the problem was certainly not about any lack of innate skill. 'We negotiate every day and all the time. What it comes down to in the workplace is our own confidence in our own value.'

Many women in organisations are concerned that

asking for more means they will be seen as a bitch or aggressive, and women do tend to take work feedback too personally, she said. 'We do tend to analyse a comment to death. Some of the women I've spoken to at the senior level are comfortable with negotiating, but they are the exception, and others in senior roles don't even think they should negotiate at all.'

A first step in addressing workplace negotiation is actually 'understanding that everything is negotiable'. That includes hours of work, holidays, family care leave, telecommuting – and pay. 'Some people just don't get that, or they forget. They also need to be able to do their homework. If they know what the market pays and their competitors, and how many people in the country can do what they do, that helps.'

Alderman has been surprised by the number of executive women who don't even consider the option of talking to their boss. 'These are senior, intelligent women. What comes up time and time again is women are not comfortable with negotiating.' Negotiating skills in the workplace are developed over time, she said, so you have to practise them to become proficient.

One of the reasons academic Mara Olekalns from Melbourne Business School (MBS) became interested in women and negotiating styles was to learn more about the backlash they unwittingly unleashed by simply behaving in certain ways across the negotiating table. While she's not a believer in the idea that all women are inherently poor at negotiating, Olekalns says they do get much poorer economic and other outcomes than men. And that can be a serious problem. 'It's not their negotiating style, but things they don't do that men do.' And there's plenty of academic research to back up this conclusion.

With this knowledge as a starting point, Olekalns designed a series of workshops at MBS to help women understand what is happening when they negotiate, and why the same behaviour as men has very different consequences for women. 'Women are very concerned about dealing with someone who is very tough and the emotional element of negotiating, both how they feel and the feelings when emotions come back to them.'

But when women engage in the kinds of behaviour that leads to career success for men, they are penalised, she said. 'They get poorer performance appraisals and personal derogation. Women are undermining their chance of success.' The effect of exhibiting organisational citizenship behaviour, the kinds of things you do above and beyond the scope of your job to keep the workplace moving along, is a classic example. Men who engage in corporate citizenship behaviour are viewed very positively and there's no effect if they don't engage in that behaviour. However, women who don't get with the program get a more negative appraisal. There are, she said, different expectations about how women behave and how it prevents them from getting ahead. 'What we see very clearly from the research is it's not the kind of strategies they choose to use, but the ramifications of being contentious.'

Men in negotiations are much more likely to focus on the best possible outcomes and keep pushing for that, while women focus on the minimum that is acceptable and stop at that. And men are much more likely to go in to their manager and say, 'I have another job offer and what are you going to do about it?' Women with an alternative just walk out the door. Olekalns's message is not about teaching women to behave like men, but how to use strategies to get a fairer outcome.

> In a perfect world the system would adjust to women, but in reality women are disadvantaging themselves, and the impact is on things like their retirement savings. Women go into their first job and men increase their salary by 10 per cent and that magnifies over a 40-year career. If this is the way the world works at the moment, I want to make sure I have the same chance as the man in the next office.

Challenging traditional behaviour and redirecting negotiations to aim for a productive outcome is helpful advice. This is clearly not an easy balancing act, and simply telling women to be more pushy when pay is discussed is a massive over-simplification of a very tricky situation.

There is no question that the gender pay gap exists and has massive implications for women now and in the future. Far from being exaggerated, the research would suggest it is probably underestimated, particularly in its long-term impact. While some business leaders downplay the notion of any gap – or insist it wouldn't happen on their watch – as a society we apparently do believe this is an issue that should be addressed. A 2008 study by the Diversity Council and EOWA found that 76 per cent of Australians agreed steps should be taken to close the pay gap between men and women. The federal government's *Making it Fair* report found the same level of community support for addressing the gender pay gap.

It seems Australians understand the need to correct unfairness in theory, but there is still strong denial about the existence of a pay gap in practice, bolstered by the notion in many businesses that jobs where women dominate – feminised areas such as human resources and marketing – are of less value and are rewarded accordingly. Yet the implications of closing the gap are significant. Looking at the relationship between the gender wage gap and economic growth, NATSEM suggested closing the gender gap by just one percentage point could increase GDP by around $4.4 billion in Australia. We also have an economy that increasingly depends on self-funded retirees, and a shrinking safety net for many basic services, which means it is crucial to pay women properly for their labour and allow them to make financial provisions for their entire lives.

Myth-busting the pay gap in this context is almost a patriotic duty. If we don't really come to grips with this the problem will not resolve itself for many decades, or at all in some cases. There is no quick fix, although pay audits are an important first step. Understanding how and why the pay gap exists feeds into the foundations of other myths about women and work. Put simply, the work women do is often valued differently to men's and seen as less worthy of higher pay. Bias continues to play a part in many formal pay systems, although it is not overt. Given the tightrope that women walk with behaviour at the bargaining table, plus the impact of career breaks, their already lower salaries can often mean they remain out of step with their male peers throughout their lives.

The pressure to tackle the causes of the gender pay gap and to rectify it are gathering pace, and pressure to keep this up must be relentless. Estimates in Australia and the UK predict that if nothing changes it will take another century to reach pay parity in senior jobs. That's just too long to wait.

CASE STUDY: ST BARBARA

Goldminer St Barbara has brought in a range of new measures to attract and retain a resource that is worth its weight in gold – skilled people. The Melbourne-based, listed company has three mines and two processing plants at Leonora and Southern Cross in remote Western Australia, so amid rising gold prices there are challenges in attracting and retaining employees.

With the support of CEO Tim Lehany and the board, and under the guidance of human resources manager Katie-Jeyn Romeyn, the company has developed a diversity policy with measurable objectives and targets. It includes flexible work, special roster arrangements for employees and paid parental leave of 18 weeks. The company has boosted women's representation from 15 to 17 per cent, and women recruits have increased from 18 per cent in 2009 to 27 per cent in 2011. According to Lehany diversity is not only the right and just thing to do, it is good business. 'We've seen an enormous change in the industry – it was illegal to have women work in mines,' he said. 'We compete for resources, capital and talent. So to access a greater pool of people is part of that.'

In a sector known for having low numbers of women – only about 15 per cent of the mining workforce and 11 per cent of mining engineers – increasing female participation and leadership has long been a challenge.

St Barbara's exploration division now has 51 per cent female employees, out of a team of 21 people working in geology roles. The company has 266 permanent employees and uses contractors for underground mining, with a total workforce of about 900.

If the diversity policy were not in place there would be a lot of talented people who would not be working for St Barbara, Romeyn said. And in a skills shortage, that's a compelling reason to introduce such measures. Along with the extended paid parental leave, the company introduced a return-to-work incentive. It also provides continuity of superannuation and entitlements during parental leave – which men are also taking. 'The first thing I put forward was the parental leave guideline to our CEO to see what he thought about it,' Romeyn said. 'He was so supportive. He said, "It makes absolute business sense to tap into this talent and the costs are nothing".'

There have been tangible results in the retention of skilled employees and productivity. One example is a couple employed by the company in Marvel Loch, Western Australia. Health, safety and emergency response adviser Sally Doley and services supervisor John Bellotti work opposite ends of the roster to accommodate childcare needs and have one day off together each week. Doley returned from maternity leave in 2009, following the birth of daughter Lilley in 2008.

When people are in flexible arrangements, they work

harder and you get more bang for your buck, according to Romeyn. There is still plenty of work to be done, but the senior team now views the diversity efforts as an important part of strategy.

MYTH 3:
WOMEN DON'T WANT THE TOP JOBS

I wish I had a few dollars for every time a CEO has told me over the years that he would love to have more senior women in his team but he has discovered they really don't want the senior jobs. Usually this is followed by an anecdote about a conversation in the lift with a women executive who told him she was not interested in more responsibility and had enough on her plate. And that's it – from then on he seems to feel assured that all the women who have worked long hours and just as hard as (or harder than) their male colleagues to get up the greasy pole and hold onto a senior job really don't want any more recognition or reward. They want to stay clear of the corner office where the decisions are made, avoid the perks, the status and the power. Of course they do; all of them.

Ok, I do know some very capable and qualified women who have decided the fight is simply not worth it, or have taken a close look at what goes on in management ranks and backed right off (some men do this too, of course). It's not a decision they have made in isolation and they haven't exactly been given encouragement to aspire along the way either – often the reverse. But not all women feel this way and some are forthright enough to make their goals clear. A well-qualified woman I know had a conversation in the lift with her CEO that reversed the scenario – she asked whether there were options for promotion in her area and the CEO, taken aback, asked why she wanted a promotion? 'Because I'm ambitious,' she replied. He was clearly put off and her frank admission left him nonplussed. To date, no promotion has materialised.

It's fairly rare to hear women beyond the early stages of their career stating their ambition with such certainty. There are many women who would acknowledge they have a strong desire to have high-quality work and to earn appropriate reward and recognition for it, but they just can't identify with the overweening, back-stabbing, clawing-to-the-top-of-the-ladder version of ambition that seems to emerge when it's applied to women. That definition has never been something I could relate to, but I have realised that I am indeed ambitious if it means wanting a good job that engages and satisfies me. Asked during my career of 30 years if I was ambitious for the next rung of the ladder however, I would probably have struggled to say yes.

I think the CEOs and executives who tell me the women they know aren't ambitious find the thought comforting and convenient because it confirms their belief that the lack of women at the top is no one's fault but the women's – they are just not cut out for the high-octane jobs and have a natural inclination to focus on their family, just like the stay-at-home wives of many male CEOs. Assumptions are also made about women's tenacity and resilience for senior roles in this context too. When asked about CEO roles and women, the chair of Westpac, Ted Evans, told the *Financial Review*: 'The jobs are incredibly demanding and to find women to do these jobs is not easy'. His comments reflected the widespread belief that women as a cohort are not willing or able to take on such roles – even if they are asked.

That's a big assumption. In my experience they simply are not asked or encouraged to put their hat in the ring nearly as often as men, all the way through the ranks. They may well be on the receiving end of consistent but informal signals about the roles that aren't really for them, particularly when a job has traditionally been held by and associated with men, such as many supervisory or management jobs. The feeling that women lack the bottle to get ahead (and have too many distracting home duties anyway) seems to kick in no matter how qualified the woman is or how long and illustrious her career. And there are many traps for prominent women displaying ambition and drive too, as I will examine. In fact, ageism can actually be lethally combined with sexism in some of these cases to effectively sever a career.

I recall hearing about a senior executive team meeting at a large company when a top appointment was discussed and a 50-year-old woman's name was raised. She was quickly dismissed by one participant, who said she wouldn't have the 'energy' required for the job. It was then pointed out that the male CEO of the organisation was at least a decade older and seemed to cope. The woman discussed was eventually appointed to the role, but it would be unlikely for the assumptions made about her energy – read ambition – to have been made about a man of the same age. However, this enduring myth about ambition and gender has more to it than misunderstandings about women's capacity at senior levels.

The deep sense of unease or ambivalence women feel about expressing ambition also has a lot to do with the connotations of the word and gender norms. This can make women reluctant to even mention the 'a' word or feign indifference or aversion to it. However, when asked about their goals and plans, a different picture emerges, as research from the last few years shows. Men and women do not have materially different levels of ambition, according to a study of senior Australian executives by Bain and Chief

Executive Women in 2011. The study of mainly senior and management executives found that 74 per cent of women and 76 per cent of men surveyed aspired to leadership roles.

Similarly, women and men were found to have the same aspirations for their careers according to *Generation F*, an Equal Opportunity for Women in the Workplace Agency study that looked at females between 16 and 65 years. According to Anna McPhee, EOWA director at the time:

> Australian women – Generation F – are highly
> skilled, just as ambitious as men and want the
> opportunity to develop their skills. But persisting
> gender bias and old-school policies regarding
> flexible working conditions and work–life balance
> continue to hamper Generation F's positive
> participation in the workforce. Thirty-one
> percent of the women we spoke to say they would
> participate more in the workforce if their partners
> did more of the domestic work. Because women's
> time is sliced up more than men, it can mean they
> have less time to further their education, take
> on career progression training and networking
> which is of concern for women, but also for the
> Australian economy.

The study identified key areas where business was

falling short of what women want in the workplace: 75 per cent of Generation F wanted opportunities for promotion and progression, but only 49 per cent said their organisation provided them with this opportunity. Supportive bosses and management were important for 90 per cent of women seeking a job, but only 64 per cent said that this was true of their workplace. Only 55 per cent of women said their workplace had a good organisational record of promoting and supporting women; and just 51 per cent of women said their organisation had a large number of women in senior positions. The findings make it clear that all things being equal (theoretically, in other words) women are keen to succeed and are ambitious, but it is the reality of their lives within and outside the workplace that can have a major impact on their aspirations.

The myth of low ambition applies to women in all ranks and jobs and not just the high-fliers. When appointments and promotions are discussed double standards often apply around some of the common but highly subjective qualities considered essential for many jobs, such as confidence, drive and ambition. When there's a subtle but pervasive belief that women are somehow naturally lacking in these areas, they would have to be robots not to absorb some of this message along the way and then find that ambition is not an easy word or concept for them to negotiate. From childhood on there are subtle, and not so subtle, reminders that ambition is still at odds with femininity. Once women hit the workforce the mixed messages about overt ambition combine with plenty of informal penalties for those who behave assertively or articulate their drive. What's acceptable for men is often off-limits for women because of different standards.

According to Melbourne academic Dr Hannah Piterman in the report, *Women in Leadership*, women are expected to be selfless, while self-orientation and competitiveness are accepted in males.

> As a society, we still struggle with the notion of female authority. Women who are seen to step outside a stereotypical female paradigm can engender rage in others, both male and female. There are many extraordinary women who continue to achieve extraordinary things. However, as long as being extraordinary remains the tacit prerequisite by both men and women for women's entry into leadership, senior ranks will remain populated by men. It is undoubtedly a cultural problem and therefore cultures need to shift for female authority to thrive.

That kind of change is challenging to say the least. But it reminds us why women in all walks of life are daunted by expressing their ambition. Some years ago I discovered *Necessary Dreams*, the work of Anna Fels, who conducted a series of interviews with women and men in the business world about the fraught area of ambition. The women she interviewed hated the word ambition when applied to their own lives.

> For these women ambition necessarily implied egotism, selfishness, self-aggrandizement, or the manipulative use of others for one's own ends. These women's denial of their own ambitiousness was particularly striking in contrast to the men I interviewed, who assumed that ambition was a necessary and desirable part of their lives. Perhaps even more surprising, the very women who deplored ambition in reference to their own lives freely admitted to admiring it in men. Looking through developmental studies of both boys and girls, I noticed that they virtually always identified the same two components of childhood ambition. There was a (at least theoretically) practicable plan that involved a real accomplishment – mastery – requiring work and skill. And then there was an expectation of approval: fame, status, acclaim, praise, honor.

However, it is simplistic to assume that there is one clear reason for these attitudes, as the reality is far more complex. Fels found that many women did indeed feel uncomfortable about using the word 'ambition' in relation to themselves. Many of the problems they encountered in their careers were about interrupted tenure, or barriers that were mostly due to organisations being structured around the 'male life cycle'. Different types of career paths were rarely tolerated or rewarded in these strictly linear structures, which were also age-sensitive and reflected highly competitive 'up or out' workplaces.

It doesn't usually start out this way, with young women's ambition dissipating once they enter the workforce. They succumb to powerful cultural imperatives that equate ambition and quests for recognition with lack of femininity, and many begin to associate the word with selfishness or egotism, Fels explained in 'Do women lack ambition?'. Because women receive little praise for their achievements or the qualities they have used in their work (and because it is seen as incongruent with femininity), they deny their ambition and give up on their aspirations. Similarly, a major 2008 study of civil servants by the Centre for Gender and Women's Studies at Trinity College in Dublin found that women were more ambitious than men when they started their careers. But the combination of broken career paths due to child-bearing and perceptions about ambition in women were key inhibitors. Ambitious women were seen as unfeminine and their problems started early on in their careers, due to a lack of viable career paths or role models that would suit their lives, the research found.

Although this discussion has come a long way in recent years, it's not helpful to find misconceptions about women and ambition continually being recycled with scant attention to the role of business norms. If the myth-busting surrounding ambition is going to be effective we need to be alert to the recycling of some dodgy assumptions, even in recent studies. A couple that came across my desk proved the point. A 2011 report on women and ambition, *Ambition and Gender at Work,* revealed some interesting findings, but fell into the trap of focusing on why women don't behave like men, while virtually ignoring the impact of context on behaviour.

Instead of concentrating on why women express lower levels of ambition for some roles (not all) the study concluded that women's lack of confidence and ambition are major inhibitors to their progress, ignoring the often clear messages they are sent about such aims. The study makes the error of assuming that all things are equal at work, so if women are not making it up the ladder there must be something wrong with them. Thus, the authors claim, women are offered the same development opportunities as men in organisations, whereas many women are in fact left out of performance management programs and development from early in their career, as I mentioned earlier (myth 1). But the UK study did make one thing crystal clear: the norms of what a successful manager looks like continue to reflect a traditional, male breadwinner model. It's no surprise then that some women can't summon up the ambition to replicate that.

The degree of caution that women tend to exhibit about job applications was seen as a negative in this study, although surely there is some sense in being careful about applying for a new job, particularly if you shoulder a caring role too and need some flexibility. Major research in 2008 by Harvard Business School academic Professor Boris Groysberg on star performers in Wall Street stockbroking firms and their levels of success after changing employers uncovered a very different outcome. Women's better due diligence and risk aversion about jumping ship paid off in spades for them, and, he concluded, they tended to be far more successful after moving jobs than men with similar experience and reputations. One of the other reasons for their success was their stronger relationship with and focus on their clients, possibly because they found themselves excluded from a lot of the internal politics of their firm. Women were more likely to forge close bonds with their external connections, so when they did change jobs many of these clients went with them, thus contributing to greater success in their new role.

Despite a complex attitude to stating ambition, the pervasive belief that women actually rarely ask for promotions or career-enhancing options – like overseas postings – and thus destroy their chances of getting ahead, is largely a misconception, as it turns out. This conclusion has always puzzled me. Even though I am ambivalent about describing myself as ambitious, I know many feisty, experienced and well-educated women who have constantly put their hand up for opportunities or job openings and I can't imagine I am alone in seeing this in my workplace all the time. But somehow the idea that women as a cohort are not putting themselves forward for any new roles at all persists, and helps buoy the myth that they lack ambition.

According to Catalyst's study, *The Myth of the Ideal Worker*, doing all the right things to get ahead worked well for men, but did not provide as great an advantage for women. It was found that commonly used career strategies, such as letting the boss know you are ready for the next step, that you are willing to put in extra time and effort, and networking up the ladder had little bearing on the rate at which senior women advanced to leadership. By looking at post-MBA job changes and salary levels of men and women, Catalyst found that women do ask for salary rises and, despite perceptions to the contrary, are not seeking slower career tracks. When the study was released Catalyst CEO, Ilene Lang, commented: 'This study busts the myth that "women don't ask". In fact, they do. But it doesn't get them very far. Men, by contrast, don't have to ask.' Even in the most pro-active group studied, twice as many men as women advanced into leadership roles. The study concluded that women need to adopt different strategies from men, not to imitate them.

Given these results, it was interesting to also read a *Harvard Business Review* blog item from around the same time: 'Four ways women stunt their careers unintentionally'. Admittedly, even the title of this article failed to excite. It makes women (and that means all of us) sound like a bunch of vapid, clueless creatures blundering through their careers without any awareness of what is happening around them. But setting that aside, guess what one of the conclusions was? Women stymie their careers because they never ask for a promotion, according to the research (by US authors and consultants Jill Flynn, Kathryn Heath, and Mary Davis Holt). 'We've seen it over and over again: women fail to get promoted because they fail to step up and apply.'

Women are also too modest, don't speak up and try too hard to blend in, they claim. This sounds perilously close to a classic female stereotype – and a long way from the Catalyst results. The interviews used for the HBR article came from men and women, so this is not only a male perception. However, the fact is that there are many more men in positions of power who have discretion over who gets the promotion, and their views about appropriate qualifications and ambition levels can make a big difference to women's career outcomes. The necessary skills to get ahead are often presented as an objective set of criteria, but many are subjective and revolve around characteristics such as assertiveness, quick decision-making and strong networking. These are a gender-biased set of terms that bear a remarkable resemblance to the stereotype of an alpha male and, as the evidence shows, what appears to work well for ambitious men going up the ladder can have a very different outcome for women.

Once they actually get to a leadership role there are so many pitfalls for ambitious women who have pursued high office that it's a wonder the few who make it are there at all. Many of us don't even realise how deeply attached to a powerful male leadership model we are, even to the extent of preferring our leaders to have deep voices and greater height than average, as a number of studies have found. Overt ambition is not just tolerated but expected from archetypal leaders, but the opposite occurs with women in these positions. I think the aversion many women have to openly expressing ambition is probably reinforced by observing the way high-profile women are treated and the torrid time they get for stepping outside gender boundaries.

As a few more women become leaders they are finding out just how difficult it is to walk the tightrope between fulfilling traditional expectations without appearing weak or unfeminine, as Prime Minister Julia Gillard has discovered. The continuing fascination with whether Gillard plotted well in advance to topple her predecessor Kevin Rudd is all about revealing those unseemly signs of naked ambition that have such severe penalties for women. I was particularly struck by the many contradictions around visibly ambitious women in high-profile jobs when both Julia Gillard and Anna Bligh were in the spotlight during the Queensland floods of 2011. Bligh's performance had little to do with her gender and more to do with her experience and an intellect that allowed her to process and communicate huge amounts of detail while sounding calm, caring and authoritative. As prime minister, Gillard stayed on the sidelines, as she should, but attracted plenty of criticism for appearing to be cold and unemotional. But here's the catch: Bligh was not overly emotional, except for tearing up at one press conference. Men do that in such circumstances too and it's perfectly understandable. It was a no-win situation for Gillard – if she had been crying openly and attracting more attention than Bligh it would not have gone down well at such a time either.

We continue to judge women harshly if they fail to show emotion and sufficient feminine traits, but are just as quick to condemn and pigeon-hole them as overly sensitive and less capable if they do. It is also telling that ambition in a woman is usually described as ruthless or even obscene, which is how New South Wales politician Frank Sartor described former premier Kristina Keneally. In the business world, CEOs such as Sue Morphet, who heads Pacific Brands, are often criticised for their impassive behavior, particularly when there is a crisis. When Pacific Brands closed a number of factories in 2009, leaving many workers redundant, there were very personal public attacks on Morphet, with one newspaper article asking how a woman could do such a thing. Westpac CEO Gail Kelly is sometimes described as remote or even too masculine in style. It's hard to imagine this particular kind of commentary being applied to senior men, who are more likely to be seen as tough operators.

Christine Nixon, the former Victorian police commissioner, also dramatically tripped over traditional gendered notions of what a leader should and shouldn't look like and a raft of double standards. Nixon was given a torrid time during the Royal Commission into the 2009 Black Saturday fires. In hindsight, she wrote in her 2011 biography, there were certainly things she would have done differently during the crisis, and 'the newspaper archive will provide rich pickings for management textbooks, for social commentators, for the gender debate, for policy wonks'. What particularly rankled with Nixon, however, was the 'questioning of my management capability'. This was particularly confronting, 'given my decades-long efforts to build and refine my skills, and the success these efforts had achieved'.

A man in Nixon's position would also have been grilled during a Royal Commission – quite rightly – but it's unlikely his legitimacy as a leader would have been called into question in quite the same way. The ridicule of Nixon's weight and the fact she went out for dinner on the night of the fires, was savage. The ABC's *Media Watch* program pointed out in mid-2011 the extraordinary level of vitriol from some media commentators and talkback callers about Julia Gillard, Sydney Lord Mayor Clover Moore and, some years ago, Liberal minister Amanda Vanstone, which tend to take on quite a different level of acidity and focus on appearance from that directed towards male politicians. That ambition, assertiveness and strength seen in men, for example, is seen as callous and uncaring for women. Instead of improving as more women move into authority, the trend seems to be continuing unabated and extensive research corroborates the phenomenon.

A 2011 US study revealed that we still associate men – and 'male' qualities – with leadership. Both

men and women still see women as being less qualified or less 'natural' in leadership roles, according
to the meta-analysis of a number of research efforts
on the topic, by Northwestern University, Illinois.
According to Liz Bolshaw, in her 'Women at the Top'
blog, women may also be seen to be presumptuous
or acting inappropriately when they adopt culturally masculine behaviour that is expected or required
for such roles. Cultural stereotypes can make it seem
that women do not have what it takes for important
leadership roles, thereby adding to the barriers they
encounter in attaining roles that yield substantial
power and authority, according to study co-author
and psychology professor, Alice Eagly. As the *Financial Times* points out, there have been many surveys
showing that, in fact, women are seen as having many
of the same attributes as men when it comes to what
makes a great leader. The exception is in the ambition and decisiveness area, which remains stubbornly
associated with men.

The media plays a major role in reinforcing these
associations. It's easy to become inured (even as a journalist with a particular focus on gender) to the sheer
level of male authority figures on the public stage. I
was fascinated and shocked by an article about the
role of women in the UK media by Kira Cochrane in
2011, 'Why is British life dominated by men?'. She
tracked the number of women writing in the media

and appearing on TV and found the numbers horribly low: in a typical month in the United Kingdom 78 per cent of newspaper articles were written by men, 72 per cent of Question Time contributors were men and 84 per cent of reporters and guests on Radio 4's Today show were men. 'Where are all the women?' she asks. When she dug into the reasons she found that a complex series of assumptions and stereotypes are hampering real change, particularly when women are highly visible to the public.

> The fewer women there are in the public eye, the more anomalous they look when they do appear. I'm often wryly amused by the male journalists who comment on how terrifying they find all-female environments ... I was struck by a quote from Martin Amis, in a recent *Observer* interview with feminist activist Gloria Steinem. When Amis met Steinem in 1984, at the offices of feminist magazine *Ms*, he wrote that he was aware of his 'otherness, my testosterone, among all this female calm'. What's rarely acknowledged is that women have to operate as 'other' on the public stage most of the time – the difference being that they could never admit this, and could certainly never confess to terror, however comic, for fear of being seen as pathetic. The marginalisation of women, as with the marginalisation of any other group,

means those who do put their head above the parapet are highly visible, and much more likely to be taken as representative of their entire sex. If a male comic performs badly on *Have I Got News for You*, he lets himself down. If one of the few women to appear performs badly, she's proof that women just aren't funny.

An Australian study of women's representation in print media, *Women in Media Report,* found a similar dearth of females. It revealed that females account for just 20 per cent of all commentary in metropolitan print media, and that in finance news the figure drops to just 10 per cent. It was commissioned by the Women's Leadership Institute Australia, which was founded by business owner and director Carol Schwartz, who told me she was fed up with the lack of women appearing in the media and as conference speakers, despite plenty of contenders. She has also set up a web register of women willing to be contacted or to speak at forums to try and counter the problem.

The scarcity of women commentators and experts in the media despite the increasing number of contenders is not a benign case of ignorance. There's strong resistance and double standards around women with ambition and leadership credentials and, according to Hannah Piterman, 'a deep level of cultural resistance to female authority'.

> While the ability to adapt is a skill many
> successful leaders share, women need greater
> space to exercise authenticity if they are to be
> truly effective leaders. They need to command
> respect and loyalty from their colleagues in
> order to achieve significant and sustainable
> outcomes for business. To this end a greater
> acknowledgement of the different look of female
> authority is needed.

The ambitious woman is often trapped between a male paradigm and an unpalatable female stereotype, Piterman found. Corporations addressing gender inequity usually see female attributes and behaviour as the problem, so much time and energy is invested in remedial programs and mentoring to make women 'a better cultural fit within a male dominated environment'. This gives women 'stilts to play on an uneven playing field but doesn't flatten out the field itself'. The very emotion we demand from our female leaders is also perceived as part of a female problem with leading. Yet, as we've seen with women CEOs, the absence of obvious emotion in their management style is construed negatively too.

Critical analysis of the evidence suggests that women in the workplace don't lack ambition, but face a minefield when it comes to expressing or exhibiting it. Stepping away from the workplace gives us some other clues as to why this myth just doesn't stack up. In fact, women are often seen as driven and intensely ambitious about their appearance, their shopping, their children and their marital prospects. The keenly competitive mother or single woman desperate for a husband are stock caricatures in popular culture and, of course, often reflect unflattering and sexist stereotypes. Instead of admiring those women who exhibit classic ambition and use tactics to reach a goal, the woman hunting for a husband is branded conniving and manipulative. Nevertheless, these portrayals do not assume women innately lack such qualities, rather they are seen as having too much ambition and often for unworthy or superficial goals (despite the social pressure to be thin, beautiful and the perfect mother of over-achieving children).

Back in the workplace, organisations can do something about changing these dynamics around ambition and gender. Modelling appropriate behaviour from the top, providing extra support for women who move into senior roles and working towards a critical mass of women (around 30 per cent) at all levels can make a big difference. These are shifts that would accommodate a women's ability to legitimately exhibit ambition without fear of penalties. In Australian workplaces there is still a strong bias to the good mother versus good worker ideals, outlined by federal Sex Discrimination Commissioner Elizabeth Broderick in the *Gender Equality Blueprint*, which makes it particularly difficult for women to articulate, aspire to or successfully plan for senior level careers. Many women clearly find the articulation of their career goals a much less straight-forward task than men, and including women in management development from graduate intake levels while harnessing early career ambition appear to be important levers to break this cycle.

My analysis of women's desire for advancement and their relationship with ambition would suggest that many of us are still uncomfortable with this word, but our reaction is dependent on just how it is defined and in what context it is applied. We are surrounded by constant reminders in the media, workplace and popular culture that women are not suitable leaders and are breaking a taboo when they stick out their necks. High profile is high danger when it comes to women in power. Busting the myth is dependent on breaking the traditional link between authority and maleness, thus validating a different model that normalises female ambition, instead of using it as a veiled insult. As more brave women slowly start to take on leadership roles in business and government, the old assumptions about who has what it takes might finally focus on a woman's ability and charisma and not how she looks.

CASE STUDY: NORTON ROSE

A determined effort at law firm Norton Rose Australia has resulted in the number of women making partner-ship rising in just a few years from 9 to 22 per cent. Sally Macindoe, a partner and head of the firm's environment and planning practice, helped lead the charge for more gender equity at the firm. The focus on diversity began in 2005, and since then the firm has doubled the number of women working flexibly and increased the rate of return of women from parental leave from 50 per cent to 81 per cent.

The progress helped earn Macindoe a gong at the 2011 Equal Opportunity for Women in the Workplace Agency Business Achievement Awards, and while it didn't happen overnight, it is proof that change is pos-sible. That's not the usual message from many of the large law firms, which acknowledge they have a gender equity problem, but then claim they have had no success addressing it. Some of this needs deep cultural change to make it happen, and Macindoe said Norton Rose has invested a huge effort in this and there's still heaps to do. But she had learnt that the change has to be a com-bination of heart and head, of using data to back up an appeal to logic.

> A couple of years ago I had a conversation with a
> partner close to me who asked if I really thought it

was good for me being so closely associated with the issue. That's when I realised they still haven't understood this is a business issue – they think it is a social policy issue. I decided to get the business case costed for turnover of female staff. I talked to the partners about that and that was a huge turning point.

Her costings were conservative, partly because it's hard to measure the full impact when women leave, due to intangibles such as the effect on relationships with clients. But it did the trick and attention started to focus on the actual effects of the exodus of skilled women. Although the senior leadership of the firm was on board, the partners still needed convincing, and Macindoe discovered that one way to hit them between the eyes was to outline how many billable hours they would have to work to make up the shortfall when a woman left. Macindoe herself is a role model, having worked flexibly for 14 years while building her career. 'It helps me do a bit of myth-busting,' she says. 'I've been promoted to partner and kept going up the ranks. It's just not true that you can't keep progressing professionally.'

MYTH 4:
WOMEN WITH CHILDREN DON'T WANT A CAREER

My brother was listening to a talkback radio program one day about the failure of many women lawyers to make partnership in law firms, despite entering the profession in ever-increasing numbers. Several callers and commentators made the point that women's child-bearing years overlapped with a critical career period, thus leaving them at a disadvantage, which most of them saw as insurmountable. He listened for a while, increasingly incredulous. 'Haven't women always had children?' he asked me as he recounted the conversation later. 'Surely,' he said, 'these law firms could adjust their practices and career paths to reflect this fact?'

Well, yes they have and they could. Women have been entering the workforce for a fair few decades now and pouring out of universities and higher education too. But structurally we may as well be stuck in the 1950s for all the adjustments that have been made to social attitudes about family responsibilities – although at least these days women don't have to resign when they get married or announce their pregnancy. Nevertheless, when women do have kids the penalties in the workplace can be swift and severe, and self-reinforcing of attitudes about female involvement in the workplace in general.

Motherhood bias can be brutal and blatant. In a well-known study on the topic, 'Getting a job: Is there a motherhood penalty?', Stanford University academic Shelley Correll and co-author Stephen Benard conducted a laboratory experiment in which participants evaluated application materials for a pair of same-race, same-gender, ostensibly real-job applicants who were equally qualified, but differed on parental status. I often cite this study when speaking at forums because it never fails to draw a gasp of surprise and horror from the audience.

Correll and Benard found that, '[r]elative to other kinds of applicants, mothers were rated as less competent, less committed, less suitable for hire, promotion and management training, and deserving of lower salaries'. They were also held to stricter performance standards, while men were not penalised for being parents and appeared to benefit from having children on some measures. 'At some level, there is still a perceived incompatibility between family and the workplace, which disadvantages mothers', Correll told the Clayman Institute for Gender Research in 2009. 'Organisations may be making errors in judgment based on stereotypical assumptions that prevent them from hiring the best person for the job.' Another finding was that while mothers were often perceived as not working hard enough, when they did work hard, they were seen as unlikeable and selfish. You really can't win that one, can you?

Some of the reaction is linked to traditional ideals about parenting and a lingering sense that women with kids have made their bed (all the beds probably) and should lie in it. I once heard the decision to have a family described as a lifestyle choice, which rather neatly reflected this idea that raising a family was just like buying an expensive appliance – a little show-offy and selfish. Or a bit like a mild infection that you keep picking up. And goodness, us girls just can't seem to kick the habit, can we? Oh, there is the need to perpetuate the human race and all that, and on the other hand, the over-the-top reaction if women happen to remain childless (although little of this judgement is directed at men with or without kids). You only have to think about the furore over Julia Gillard's empty kitchen and the fact that her lack of children has made her the target of several offensive and barbed comments in public – and many more in private, no doubt. We are still vaguely suspicious of women who don't have children, but not so much of men, and as a friend pointed out to me, there's an assumption that all childless women have made a deliberate decision about the matter, when in fact a host of reasons could be involved. A rock and a hard place comes to mind.

When I speak about this issue at forums or in the column it's clear from the response that many mothers have at least encountered some form of conscious or thoughtless judgement. And many of them tell me that the experience converted them into feminists. In fact, Elizabeth Broderick, the federal Sex Discrimination Commissioner, often talks about how her awareness was raised when she had a family. Up until her conversion – she dubs it 'late onset feminism' – she believed nothing would hamper her career path at a law firm, so the effect was a shock and an incentive to make things change. Sadly, the punitive attitudes to mothers means that there's still a lot of maternity discrimination around, most commonly involving a 'restructuring' while the employee is on maternity leave that can leave them out of a job. This only got worse during the financial crisis when any deviation from full-time workloads was seen as indulgent. It's so much easier to let someone go when you think they are having a paid break and they really shouldn't come back to a job anyway.

This is why traditionalists have little patience with the struggle mothers encounter when blending paid and unpaid work, because they believe most women belong at home and can only be effective in one role at a time. Blithely ignoring the financial imperative to have a job, there's an assumption, usually covert in the workplace, that if women with kids are struggling they should get out of the workplace and leave it to those who are unencumbered. Many a CEO has told me that motherhood is the only major problem for women in the workforce and no other kind of discrimination really occurs or inhibits them.

Hmm, that qualifies as a convenient excuse if ever I've heard one. As a mother of three I would be the last person to suggest that parenting has no toll on a woman's paid job, and sleep pattern, but the statistics on women's representation in Australian businesses are so poor it doesn't make sense to conclude that all the problems arise from motherhood. Children do grow up and careers last for 45 plus years. I think the attitudes towards mothers in the workplace are but one aspect of broader gender discrimination that kicks in from the time a woman enters it, as I pointed out in myth 1. Despite the claims that having kids typically ruins a woman's career trajectory as they take long periods of leave and switch to part-time hours, the reality is a bit different. Many women have contacted me over the years to describe their experience of taking a limited amount of maternity leave only to return to full-time work and discover they have become persona non grata, have mysteriously disappeared from interesting projects, the promotions list or are forgotten when the important meetings occur.

In fact, women with small children are still battling for fundamental changes, such as scheduling meetings for time slots that accommodate their obligations. In early 2012 it was reported that NSW Labor MP Tania Mihailuk, who has three children aged six and under, had asked members of the legislation review committee to delay their regular 8.30 am meetings by 15 minutes so she could drop her children at school and childcare. The committee's deputy chairman, Geoff Lee, Liberal MP for Parramatta, refused, and told parliament: 'I know the member for Bankstown is upset with the 8.30 am meeting time. From my experience of business life ... I do not think 8.30 is too early to start. We all live busy lives, but we all make a commitment to come to Parliament.' Apparently the meetings often only run for five minutes or so. Simple and helpful as these adjustments can be they are still resisted.

No matter how good the quality of their output, mothers face an uphill battle with this behaviour, pitted against generic negative perceptions about good mums and good workers, and how never the twain shall meet. On the other hand, when it comes to male employees, the quality of their parenting, indeed their parenting status itself, is usually not part of the workplace equation and certainly has little bearing on how their performance is assessed. The revolution that opened the door to the workplace for women didn't quite deliver in the home or caring realms, as a number of commentators have pointed out, including the authors of *Time Bomb*:

> The fruit of the post 1970s second wave women's liberation has been women's right – now indeed a requirement – to join men in their work citizenship …The 'culture of mateship and the fair go, hard work and respect' that Prime Minister Gillard suggests arrives with work, does not quite reach to the fair redistribution of domestic work, the elimination of wage discrimination, the underpayment of carers, the removal of sexual harassment at work or the double load.

Data from the AWALI 2010 survey show that Australian women are participating in the workforce at a higher rate while continuing to shoulder traditional home duties, obviously putting them under increased pressure. The survey also found that women in professional occupations had worse work–life interference than their male colleagues, even when their hours were similar. The factors that create time strains and pressures for working women are well documented: lack of quality, accessible, affordable childcare, inflexibility at work, unsupportive cultures, disincentives in the wages, benefits and taxation systems, and inequality in time spent on childcare and domestic work at home.

Outside the workplace there has been some shift in the social status of parenting over the last decade or two. These days dads can happily publicly show off their skills in parenting compared to the expectations of fathers a generation or two ago. In those days fathers would have flown to the moon rather than walk to the local shops with a baby in a harness strapped to them. But that was a change that primarily loosened the parameters for men, particularly as changes in the divorce laws meant increasing numbers of separated dads were caring for their children on their own. For mothers there's been less of an upside, whether at home, where they might get a few hours to themselves on a weekend, or at work, where they are still seen as the parent who usually does the school run. It is terrific that fathers are more involved with their kids, but it hasn't challenged the idea that women are the proper guardians of home and hearth, and dad will do for a bit of bonding time.

The reciprocal change in viewing mothers as legitimate income earners has been much slower to emerge and tends to move in fits and starts. Clearly, that recognition will not occur in the workplace unless there's a redistribution of work at home too, which means women are not regarded as the default housekeepers. I have noticed an interesting element in the debate about the housework (and you can't often say that) – those who typically don't lift a finger at home are often the fiercest defenders of the sanctity of the job. I reckon anyone who thinks unrelenting full-time housework and childcare are rewarding is mostly the person who gets to choose whether they change the nappies or clean the toilet.

And yes, women are still doing most of the household and caring work for children or other family members. The popular belief that child-rearing duties are becoming more equally shared is not matched by the reality, according to research by Lyn Craig, an associate professor from the University of New South Wales' Social Policy Research Centre. She set out to uncover how parents are dividing their time between paid work, child care and housework, and found that in 62 per cent of households with children under the age of 11 both parents were in paid work. However, in almost 70 per cent of those households the father worked full-time and the mother worked part-time, retaining the major responsibilities for child-rearing and domestic chores.

Craig's research found that strategies, such as women working from home or becoming self-employed, didn't make much difference. Although she did find that in some situations fathers are taking a more hands-on approach to parenting, in what Craig refers to as 'tag-teaming' – where fathers work conventional hours while mothers work evenings and weekends. Where this was the case there was more of a gender balance, but very much at the expense of the time a couple could spend together.

What a lot of hypocrisy emerges when it comes to valuing and recognising this 'invisible' caring and domestic work. Pious commentary about a proposed reduction in the federal government's baby bonus in late 2011 included critics labelling the cuts a 'moral judgement' against stay-at-home mothers. As if our society doesn't already make a stack of judgements about these women – most of which are negative, although we'd die rather than admit it. Those who speak in sanctimonious tones about the glory of homemaking and caring roles are those who can also afford to sustain a household on one income, which is not a viable option for most Australians.

The domestic work done in homes remains largely out of sight and mind and is undervalued because it is still seen as a woman's domain. And it's not as though women are given much choice in the matter, despite the rhetoric from some commentators. Clearly, most men aren't exactly queuing up to do their share, even when paid work is equally shared. Women in paid work can't get a break even if their household can afford to outsource the cleaning or caring. Over the last few years a strange argument has arisen that feminists (notice the assumption that women make this decision) can't employ a cleaner or nanny because it represents subjugation of another woman – handily ignoring the fact cleaners and nannies are paid and some are male, of course. Employing a gardener or electrician is fine but not a cleaner. Go figure.

Meanwhile, it's still social leprosy at a party to tell someone your main job is running a family or a household. We certainly don't seem to attach much status to this crucial role. In the workplace most women find it best to keep their struggles to blend paid and unpaid work to each other or risk being labelled a whinger or a bludger if they take maternity leave and work flexible hours. They also battle perceptions they are getting away with something and that maternity leave is a holiday. Actually, maternity leave isn't like that. It's full-time (24 x 7) labour and utterly exhausting – which doesn't mean it's not rewarding. But all too often women remain quiet about the reality because if they speak up they are seen as victims who should just stay at home and look after their children anyway.

The motherhood myth relies on far too much unchallenged nonsense about the effects of maternity leave and part-time work on productivity and the economy. Research by EOWA shows that women take an average of only one year off in total from paid work for maternity leave. When I asked the

HR manager of a large financial service organisation how many employees were away in a given year on maternity leave, she said it was consistently about 3 per cent. That's right – probably far fewer than is assumed, and less than those on some other form of long service leave. And it's the same with retention rates of women coming back from maternity leave, which are assumed to be far lower than suggested by the actual evidence – many businesses now have return-to-work rates of more than 90 per cent. However, left unchecked these misconceptions work to effectively reinforce the idea that mothers are a bad bet and unreliable to boot. Lurking not too far under the surface is the feeling they are either likely to have another baby or leave anyway, no matter what the evidence reveals.

Given the gender breakdown on unpaid work it's easy to understand why women are often trying hard to bridge two demanding roles. I think there's still plenty of judgement from men and women if mums appear to be struggling in this juggling act and dropping a few balls – or the baby. (Of course, when mothers are seen as super-achievers they are called superwomen and accused of setting a bad example for ordinary women.) I know scores of mothers who have come up against judgemental teachers, workmates and partners who reinforce the idea that a job and motherhood are incompatible. Many of them believe

Contra Costa County Library
Antioch
9/12/2018 11:37:34 AM

- Patron Receipt -
- Renewals -
): 21901024558334

em Number: 31901052027853
itle: 7 myths about women and work
Renewed
)ue Date: 10/24/2018 11:37:29 AM

All Contra Costa County Libraries will be
closed on Monday, October 8th for an All Staff
Training Day. Book drops will be open. Items
may be renewed at ccclib.org or by calling
1-800-984-4636, menu option 1. In addition,
the Brentwood Library will close on September
14th, at 5:00 pm and reopen in a new building
at 104 Oak St. on Sept 29th. Please return
materials to an alternate location during this
closure. El Sobrante Library remains closed for
repairs.

it is perfectly reasonable to have their commitment to their kids questioned because of their investment in a job, and vice versa. I think we have to really work at eradicating this pernicious form of guilt. Would a man ever be accused of 'having it all' because he holds down a job and has a family? It's inconceivable (pardon the pun). Time and again I have seen men complimented for leaving work early to pick up the kids from school, while mothers feel pressure to shut up and slink away from work in case they are seen.

For some mothers, confronting this judgement and the juggling act is just too hard. I have many friends who found that looking after children in their early years was incompatible with their job demands and understandably decided to step out of the work-force. However, what is often overlooked is that many of these women have subsequently regretted severing their ties with paid work because they find it well-nigh impossible to get back into the workforce or are left with little choice but poorly paid casual jobs. They make up what is known as the under-employed and represent a significant waste of skills. But the decisions they made all the way through their child-caring years were not really choices in the true sense of the word. Their workplaces were not exactly helping them to combine the roles of mother and paid employee, and neither, in many cases, were their partners. With that lack of encouragement, and an expectation of gratitude for any accommodation, it's not surprising many of them would agree that being a decent carer and a paid worker is not possible. It's hard to imagine how much difference a more even playing field and less pressure to be a perfect mother would make to changing that belief.

It can be quite surprising – and depressing – to take a broader look at the extensive research and academic literature in this area. The 'maternal wall' is a term coined by US author and commentator Joan Williams to describe the effects of the stereotyping applied to mothers in the workforce and how this narrows their options. It can take the form of negative competence assumptions about carers and part-time workers, Williams says, and particularly mothers returning to the workforce after childbirth, plus bias assumptions. A number of US websites (such as momsrising.org) and books have started to focus on the economic effects of the maternal wall, particularly on pay.

It's a worrying trend, because it often leads to mothers with skills needed in the workplace being sidelined, as well as underpaid. Efforts by some companies to introduce flexible work schedules are increasing, but are not evenly applied, and many US surveys on flexible work hours have found they are restricted to working full-time hours but 'saving' time to earn a day off. Yet the rhetoric about 'family-friendly' companies continues and needs to be carefully examined. Some sceptics believe the business awards for this kind of activity actually hinder rather than help in changing workplaces because they recognise a suite of policies that may not be used much or continue to reinforce the so-called 'mummy track'.

So while flexible work sounds like the answer, it brings dilemmas too. I mentioned that women returning to full-time work after having children still encounter discriminatory attitudes, but much more often in Australia women returning to work after child-bearing are in flexible arrangements. Nearly half the women in paid work in Australia work less than 35 hours a week and while that represents a solution on the one hand, it also has a downside. More than half of women working part-time do not have access to paid sick leave or holiday entitlements, and, as pointed out by the authors of *Time Bomb*, by 'manoeuvring their care responsibilities around their work participation many workers, especially women workers, "step down" to lower status, lower paid jobs with fewer entitlements and benefits'.

Certainly, disruption to established working hour norms continues to be regarded by many employers as a basic impediment to career progress, despite rhetoric around more inclusive workplaces. In 'The effect of motherhood on wages and wage growth', Tanya Livermore and co-authors cite data in Australia that confirm a motherhood wage penalty of about 5 per cent for one child and 9 per cent for two or more children. The penalty emerges over time due to reduced wage growth rather than an immediate reduction post-children. Many mothers returning to work also report that their career prospects suffer and they are no longer offered the same opportunities as other male or female childless colleagues. The part-time model is so associated with the mummy track that even the occasional man who takes it will find they are shunted out of the running for promotions too. I recall hearing a male lawyer with a disabled child talking about his experience as a flexible worker and finding the same pattern of being ignored or left out of meetings as his female colleagues.

These stereotypes also mean the full-time model is seen as obligatory for men, which has a distinct downside too, especially when ageism strikes. A 2012 survey for the Financial Services Council found that three in ten of the surveyed workers aged 50 and over had suffered from age discrimination. The study's author, Nicholas Wright, said the problem of age discrimination was most stark among those in the 'middle' of the Australian workforce, particularly white-collar men. Inflexible employer attitudes that saw white-collar men as 'full-time or nothing' contributed to the problems of unfair treatment and early retrenchment of older workers, the study says. 'If a 54-year-old male accountant requested to work three days a week it would probably be denied,' Mr Wright said. On the other hand, Adele Horin recounted in 'White-collar men facing age discrimination' that the study found some older men were unwilling to accept a drop in pay or status, even as they expressed the desire for more flexible arrangements.

The stigma surrounding part-time work as a female ghetto that stunts career prospects so horrifies some women that they refuse to even consider flexible options. As one professional woman told me, she preferred to battle on with long hours and the bulk of the caring role to avoid the stigma, but to her shock she still found herself confronting stereotypes. Soon after accepting a promotion while her children were young she was asked if she felt guilty for not spending time with her family. This is a classic no-win situation – the woman got the promotion, but also the stress of the job and most of the family responsibility (there had been no shift in labour demarcation in her home as a result of her steps up the career ladder).

At the top end of business the assumption also lingers that motherhood and a career are incompatible and even make for a lethal combination. So it's interesting to note that most of the women running Fortune 500 companies in the US are parents. In 2010 there were only 15 of them and 11 have children. In Australia, five out of the six women chief executive officers of ASX200 companies in 2011 have children, and some of them have more than one child. On that basis it appears having children could even be seen as a prerequisite for women wanting the top job, and having a supportive partner comes in handy – just as it does for male CEOs. While a family is not an impediment for a high-flying male executive, different considerations come into play when it's a woman. Of course, these particular CEOs are high-achieving women, but it's still interesting that motherhood, which is so often assumed to be a reason why women don't want promotions or secondments, has not held them back.

Nevertheless, the idea lingers that well-educated women with children tend to opt out of senior jobs at some stage, leaving their employers in the lurch and wasting their expensive education. It created a real stir in 2003 when US journalist Lisa Belkin wrote her article 'The opt-out revolution'. Data she gathered from surveying a group of graduates from Harvard Business School showed that just 38 per cent of female MBAs were working full-time about 20 years after graduation. She concluded that more well-educated women were leaving work to spend time with their kids and there was a 'told you so' response from many quarters. The problem with this research was that while it did uncover a trend with this cohort (there are some reasons for this, which I will come to), the findings were then seen as applicable to all professional women and no attention was paid to the role of the workplace.

Debunkers soon pointed to statistics in the United States that showed a very small increase in the number of women with young children who were not working. In 'Are women opting out? Debunking the myth', US economist Heather Boushey concluded that the data stand in opposition to the media frenzy on this topic and for women in their thirties with professional or advanced degrees, there was no statistically significant change in job status. 'In spite of personal anecdotes highlighted in various news stories, women are not increasingly dropping out of the labour force because of their kids. The main reasons for declining labour force participation rates among women over the last four years appears to be the weakness of the labour market.'

Unfortunately the message about women leaving the office to rock the cradle was absorbed and is still circulated, although luckily with less frequency these days. I was astonished to find it alive and well when I interviewed the CEO of a large financial services organisation a couple of years ago and asked him why he struggled to retain senior women with many years of service. 'Look out there,' he said, gesturing to the window. Bewildered, I looked out the window. 'With such lovely weather in Sydney', he said, 'why would women with families hang around in an office if they could afford to leave?' Dumbfounded, I asked if he felt that way about his job, which he laughed off.

The bias he displayed about mothers in the workplace – low commitment, poised to fly the coop, happier at home, and so on – continues to stymie different workplace models and norms from really catching on. Clearly not all women want the corner office and some do take time out for child-raising, but on the other hand, the idea that women with family responsibilities by default lack career aspirations is not accurate either (see myth 3). It simply defies commonsense to think that women with long careers suddenly discover they are unable to blend caring and paid work and, in fact, data show that most of the women who leave jobs do so for exactly the same basic reasons as men.

The top five reasons both men and women have for leaving their jobs are the same, according to a 2008 survey, *Work Flexibility*, of 1600 Australian men and women, by the Equal Opportunity for Women in the Workplace Agency. The top reasons were 'I wanted to make more money'; 'Was difficult for me to progress'; 'Poor work conditions'; 'Career change' and 'Lack of clear career development'. A 2009 study conducted by Melbourne Business School associate professor Isabel Metz, in which she interviewed 44 senior female bank employees about why they left their jobs, found that five of them (11 per cent) named family responsibilities. Organisational change, such as downsizing was by far the chief reason (85 per cent). Almost half (45 per cent) indicated that unfriendly work–family practices didn't give them a fair opportunity to continue working for the organisation, which shows how critical policies such as part-time work and flexible hours are to retaining women (and men) with family commitments.

Most women leave one job for another or start their own business and don't all vanish from the workforce. In 2012 the Australian Women Chamber of Commerce and Industry found that 78 per cent of women running their own businesses were previously employed in middle to upper management. Sounds as though banging the head against the glass ceiling and battling unhelpful practices is far more likely to be the reason for shifting jobs than the difficulties of juggling childcare or coping with mother guilt.

Of course, it's also really expensive and inefficient to let experienced employees walk out the door after years of training and investment, particularly when compared to the much smaller costs or reorganising involved in accommodating them. When law firm Norton Rose (case study, myth 3) started to look at this equation they found it was not only costly, but that they could risk losing clients and overburdening the other professional staff, who would have to make up the billable hours. Partner Sally Macindoe worked out the extra hours the partners at the firm would have to work if a woman left, particularly mothers, and it was an eye opener for them. The firm has introduced a number of processes to allow women to work part-time as partners and in the last few years retention of mothers has increased, as has the number of women partners.

It's worth noting that firms like this, which are having some success in countering the motherhood myth, are not trying to change the women but are turning their sights to altering organisational practices to help retain women. Some sectors seem to be less inclined to do this and, oddly enough, they tend to be the most prestigious and highly paid. When I was asked to write a white paper on gender and the workplace for the Financial Services Institute of Australia (FINSIA) in 2010 I came across some fascinating in-depth research on motherhood and finance professionals from the United States. The financial services sector has a particular problem with women who attempted to blend paid and unpaid work, and research from Harvard academics Claudia Goldin and Lawrence Katz and colleagues in the *Harvard and Beyond Project* found that the influx of highly educated US workers into finance in the last two decades has been at a cost that fell mainly on women. They concluded that among elite white-collar jobs, finance seemed to be a particularly difficult field for anyone who was trying to combine work and family.

The impact of career breaks on women in professional roles in financial services has also been part of the study by Goldin and Katz, who surveyed 6500 Harvard and Radcliffe graduates from various classes between 1969 and 1992, and 'found that women who had gone on to earn an M.B.A. after graduating from Harvard were far less likely to be employed and have children at the time of their fifteenth reunion than were female respondents holding M.D. degrees'.

Investment banking, in particular, is more difficult for women with children than other demanding sectors such as medicine or law, according to the research, which corroborates the Belkin article. While these are US studies it is reasonable to assume that similar factors are at play for women in such jobs in Australia. My research in this area has found that at entry level the number of women graduates applying to investment banks in Australia has actually dropped in recent years, with many choosing to join law or accounting firms instead. They have been put off by the lack of women employed in these banks, which are seen as particularly aggressive, testosterone-ridden environments.

Asked about female CEOs and motherhood in the United States, Goldin said these women were clearly high achievers who could handle big challenges. They are, in other words, extraordinary. It's often the case that women executives have a stay-at-home partner and have actually adopted the sole breadwinner model to make it all work. They tend to cope by quarantining their family situation rather than blending the roles and normalising different models. They are seen as successes despite their children, which is not a judgement applied to male CEOs, whose family status is very much accepted as the norm.

At a forum to launch some research on gender by Bain and Company and Chief Executive Women in Sydney in late 2011, Westpac director and former Lion Nathan boss Gordon Cairns said the gender inequity problem in business is about those women who are not necessarily the high-fliers. We focus on exceptional women who do exceptionally well because they are exceptional, he said. His point was there are many others out there in the ranks with plenty to contribute who are not getting a fair go either, and encounter a range of barriers stemming from the motherhood myth, regardless of the hours they work or the results they achieve.

The presumptions made about mothers and their commitment to the job happens at all levels and prevents individuals from even getting the chance to discuss their intentions. This can stymie a woman's options without her ever even knowing she had them. A senior executive told me he was involved in appointing an executive to an offshore role, but when the shortlist of applicants was drawn up not one woman was included on it, despite the organisation employing several excellent women candidates. When he raised the issue he was told it was assumed no woman would want to take the job as it involved moving overseas. The job was eventually offered to a woman with children, who immediately accepted.

Given all the roadblocks encountered by mothers in their jobs after reproducing, it's a shame social pressure to be the perfect mum hasn't exactly eased off either. What I find irritating about this debate is the underlying and judgemental views about the proper way to raise kids and the almost overwhelming tendency to sheet home the responsibility to women. And I do love a brave woman who takes on the hypocrisy of all this moralising. That hideous creature the helicopter parent was big news when the New York writer Lenore Skenazy visited Australia in October 2010. Skenazy, in case you have forgotten, wrote a column in 2008 (and then a book) about letting her nine-year-old son make his own way home on the subway. All hell broke loose.

Her point was that an overprotective parenting style has not actually been in the best interests of children. It's a worthwhile argument, but almost as interesting is the vehemence of the response. Everyone seemed to have an opinion and the gloves were off.

The fracas made one point very clear: parenting standards are now deemed to be much higher than they were a few decades ago. It's dangerous to extrapolate from your own experience, but here goes, anyway. As the product of a stay-at-home mother, I can only recall the odd query about homework or exam timetables, and very little desire to dictate where we spent our afternoons – although Australian suburbia in the 1960s was not exactly downtown New York. We were a small family in our neighbourhood, with only four kids. As a result, not only were we left to our own devices a lot more than we would be now, but many mothers were running the home virtually unassisted, with more to do and fewer gadgets than today, thus they were pretty busy with cleaning and cooking (and quietly going bonkers – but that's another story).

Aside from the points Skenazy raised about the skyrocketing fear of stranger danger despite falling crime rates, another massive change has been occurring while the bar kept lifting for parents. The last generation or two has seen women's workforce participation steadily on the increase, in Australia and the United States, while family size has shrunk. That means most mothers are out of the home earning money for at least part of the week, and parental angst is being concentrated on fewer kids. It's easy to forget what a relatively recent development this is and what a radical transformation of centuries of social order it represents. Indeed, it seems the unease and disruption to traditional family dynamics from women's entry into the job ranks is actually contributing to ratcheting up parenting standards.

It's not as counter-intuitive as it may sound. As I have examined, women with children are often made to feel they shouldn't really be in the workforce if they want to raise decent human beings. That's what the so-called 'mummy wars' are all about – the well-worn idea that being a good mother and a good employee are incongruent. Guilt and fear about failure to be a good parent/worker can add up to even more performance anxiety about these roles. Perhaps it's time to reiterate why having a job and a family is actually a good idea, rather than a reason to feel horribly guilty and a failure on both fronts.

First, there's the financial factor. Many women support themselves and their families, so it's time we got over the idea that women's work is discretionary. Having two incomes is less risky and building up retirement savings is essential for all of us. Second, who deemed a stay-at-home mother the gold standard? Surely sound parenting is about quality, not quantity. For hundreds of years women did not have much time with their children, either because they were busy working in the fields or, if money allowed, the offspring were looked after by a nanny or sent to boarding school. And last, there's the housework.

Sure, women continue to shoulder the lion's share, but at least some of us have to compress it or take shortcuts, and less time spent cleaning toilets is a step forward. Skenazy advocates loosening the apron strings, but why not have a crack at countering the guilt, lowering parenting and housework standards, and revisiting that old idea of better sharing the load?

I have another suspicion that ties in with the notion our track into the workforce has been accompanied by higher standards for parenting. I wonder if all the palaver these days over the perfect partner, engagement and wedding, aside from being a commercial windfall for all sorts of commercial interests and retailers, is also part of a reaction against the moves to modernise and make fairer the institution of marriage and its labour arrangements? And that would also explain the return by young women to the habit of happily changing their surnames when they marry these days. What's that about? We thought we'd moved on from all that in the '80s, but it's back with a vengeance.

There are just a couple more elements to the motherhood myth that are not often mentioned in polite society but that should be stated. It has often seemed to me that bolstering the motherhood bias and sidetracking mothers has a really handy effect. It gets rid of some of the competition women represent from our increasingly competitive workplaces. I have seen a lot of fairly ordinary men get a step up the ladder after a talented female peer started a family, and the problem is you just don't catch up from those derailments, as researchers have found time and again. In a dog-eat-dog world the chance to step into a role or get some extra runs on the board while a colleague is away can be very tempting.

It's worth remembering too that despite all the talk of generational change, many of the men making it to senior ranks have only been able to get there because they have a dedicated stay-at-home partner who keeps the hearth warm. This kind of male breadwinner model is sometimes reversed for senior women, but it is not the answer in the long term. The fact is many executive men are in traditional marriages and unable to really empathise with women trying to combine job and family. They sometimes judge them harshly because they forget most of us don't want to or can't cope financially in that arrangement anymore. When these men are grappling with these issues they may be quite personally confronted. Myth-busting by providing some contrary views and targeting preconceptions about motherhood is not the way to win friends and influence people at work, but it's needed more than ever.

Many of us have children for a range of complex social, psychological and cultural reasons, which are rarely to do with superficial but deeply instinctive reasons. For centuries a social order operated efficiently enough for the raising of children, but women paid a significant price for that well-oiled machine. Now we are seeing an almighty struggle to produce some new frameworks that accommodate mothers – and parents – in paid jobs. Merging paid and caring work is not exactly easy, as many women know all too well, but it's made all the harder when assumptions and judgements are made about all mothers in the workplace. This is a myth that will take quite some busting because of the misunderstandings it engenders and the dodgy application of anecdotal evidence by both men and women. All too often highly subjective statements are delivered as the facts.

Motherhood does many things to a woman – it gives you scars and worries and a craving for sleep that can be demonic. It certainly changes your priorities too, just as it does for men. But it is a myth to assume all mothers lose their desire and ability to hold down a paid job, just as they don't lose their financial commitments. Make the workplace uninviting and punitive enough for mothers and they will get the message and start to believe they really shouldn't be there. Puncturing the motherhood myth has quite a lot to do with creating better workplaces and happier families, while ensuring we have future workers and consumers. It's more than worth the effort.

CASE STUDY: CSL/ASTRAZENECA

Biopharma company CSL won a 2011 EOWA business achievement award for opening an onsite childcare centre, Thinking Kids, in September 2011 after research showed that 63 per cent of employees who had taken maternity leave in 2006 did not return to work. Women make up 51 per cent of CSL's 10 000-plus employees, and the company offers flexible working options and a school holiday facility in the childcare centre.

Pharmaceutical company AstraZeneca won a similar award in 2009 for offering an onsite holiday care program for employees' children. When the details were announced at the awards the audience burst into applause – it's a simple enough idea but makes a major difference to parents.

CASE STUDY: UTS

Ross Milbourne, vice-chancellor of University of Technology, Sydney, won an award for leading CEO for the advancement of women in 2009 and mentioned a couple of measures that made a huge difference to female employees. He centralised maternity leave funding at UTS so the cost was not deducted from each faculty. This made a big difference to the way maternity leave was viewed and how women were accommodated by their workplace.

There is also a range of programs to support women at UTS and help them in career progression, including gender equity grants and women in engineering programs to help careers in non-traditional areas. Milbourne makes sure his support for the cause is visible. 'I make it an A+ priority to go to every event that encourages women's participation at the university,' he said. 'Even if I have an important meeting on, I cancel it.'

MYTH 5:
QUOTAS AND TARGETS ARE DANGEROUS AND UNNECESSARY

What a can of worms is opened when you mention these three words: quotas, women, boards. Start the discussion and within minutes a whole rash of assumptions and stereotypes are being invoked by men and women alike, with plenty of alarmist predictions about the possible consequences of introducing quotas or not. You would think it was the end of civilisation as we know it rather than a means of prising open the boardroom door a little wider. Every seminar or networking session I have attended in the last few years has discussed this subject with passion, and a fair few of the myths have surfaced too; a reminder of the potency they still hold. At the *Financial Review*'s annual Chanticleer lunch in Sydney in 2010, ANZ Banking Group chair John Morschel described legislated quotas as 'dangerous'.

I don't think they are dangerous, but I do think it's

a shame we have got to the point where we even need to discuss legislated quotas. I blame the dependency on the pipeline (myth 7) in particular for the complacency that allowed things to get so bad that legal avenues even need to be considered. The number of women on ASX200 boards, for example, decreased in 2008 to 8.3 per cent from 8.7 per cent in 2006, but due to a host of factors we will examine here, the picture has now improved, with 13.8 per cent women directors recorded in 2012.

Not all sectors have fared as poorly with board diversity as listed companies. The Australian public sector is in a slightly different position, having started focusing on this area earlier and made far more progress with women's representation. The federal government has set targets for 40 per cent women on boards by 2015. At the end of 2011, five portfolios exceeded the target, up from two portfolios in 2008–09, with seven more within 10 per cent of achieving 40 per cent. Eleven of 19 portfolios improved their representation of women on government boards and bodies in 2011.

State governments have also made better progress than the private sector, with some states aiming for 50 per cent in the next few years. But no one is deluded that the levels registered in recent years have reached giddy heights and that's exactly why quotas surfaced as a potential circuit breaker to finally trigger change.

Before looking more closely at the mythology and confusion about quotas and targets, it may help to define what they actually mean. Quotas usually refer to the legal mandating of certain numbers of board positions on listed entities to women, normally set at about 40 per cent. There is plenty of evidence to suggest that just one woman on a board is not effective for the board dynamic or the sole female. Little wonder there's a saying doing the rounds that one woman is a token, two women a conspiracy and three make a difference. While quotas are not strictly a regulation that applies solely to board appointments, so far the only countries (Norway is the most often quoted) to move to legislate in this area have restricted the regulation to directorships of listed entities and not executive or management positions within organisations. This is where targets are commonly applied, which means setting voluntary goals for certain levels of women, usually from mid-management ranks and above. Again, the range of targets vary, but somewhere between 35 and 40 per cent is common.

Targets have been introduced by a wide range of Australian companies. The pragmatists will always tell you that what gets measured gets done, and clichéd though it is, there is some truth to the adage. While quotas are fiercely resisted by many in the boardroom, targets are all the rage. The motivation for their introduction may be about avoiding further regulation and complying with new voluntary report-ing rules, rather than a rush of blood to the head about gender equity. But many believe it's at least a step in the right direction. There are some concerns about targets (I'll come back to this) unleashing a backlash, but they provide some incentive to system-atically including women candidates when appoint-ing and promoting to senior roles and keep tabs on numbers. As tackling the myths makes clear, the more evidence the better, given the role of conjecture in these discussions.

The sharp increase in formal targets provides an interesting contrast to the allergic reaction from the great and the good when the word 'quota' pops up. In fact, a range of well-known CEOs are falling over each other to endorse the use of targets. When the Male Champions of Change put out a research report in 2011, *Our Experiences in Elevating the Represen-tation of Women in Leadership*, it revealed that many corporates are in fact going down the road of informal quotas. The group includes chief country officer of Citi Australia, Stephen Roberts; former Woolworths CEO, Michael Luscombe and his replacement Grant O'Brien; Rio Tinto managing director, David Peever; Deloitte Australia CEO, Giam Swiegers; Goldman Sachs Australia chair, Stephen Fitzgerald; IBM Aus-tralia and New Zealand managing director, Andrew Stevens; Telstra's David Thodey; and Mike Smith from the ANZ.

More than half the group (54 per cent) said 'clear quantitative targets' came second in a list of the most impactful action they had taken to drive gender diversity (making the leadership team the diversity council was top of the list). 'By ensuring targets are in place, well understood and hardwired into scorecards, senior leaders get good at identifying barriers – and intervening to offset their impact. All of this adds up to improved results against the objectives.'

So it seems the opposition to quotas doesn't really apply to targets, despite being pretty similar in intent. Obviously the difference between imposed and voluntary regulation is significant. The business sector, particularly those in the top tiers, is not exactly fond of more regulation, so there's no surprise that feelings and opposition to quotas run high, but it hasn't stopped the discussion in the corporate community here and overseas. Indeed, the mere hint that this was a possibility in Australia seemed to actually help trigger some more solid action in 2010–11 than in the previous decade (as I shall examine). The Corporate Governance Council's introduction of diversity guidelines for ASX-listed companies may have happened without this discussion, but it's probably fair to say it was helped along by the suggestion that quotas could be a last resort should all else fail to budge the slow progress.

Just what are the main arguments against quotas? They seem to revolve around the belief there are not enough women to fill these roles (strangely that doesn't seem to have proved a problem so far as we'll see); as a result, the women appointed to fill the quota will not be qualified and will make an awful mess of the job. It is claimed that some sectors simply couldn't find enough women with knowledge of their business, such as resources, or with the requisite CEO or line management experience. There is a belief that good male candidates would be ignored, and as most women directors would be tokens, their failure would set back the greater cause of gender equity. Most of these overlap and are fuelled by the core concern about an adequate supply of experienced women for the job.

Those in favour of quotas refute the lack of supply objection by pointing to the number of qualified women available in a range of sectors, although this does depend on being a little less prescriptive about the kind of skills and background required for the job and searching in less traditional hunting grounds. The advocates say that is part of the reason we need quotas, because they force boards to look harder and to open up the recruitment and appointment process so that it is fairer. Once that is done and a broader suite of experience is deemed acceptable, then there will be few problems with supply to meet demand

and less risk of tokenism. Thus, they argue, there will gradually be more and more women with board credentials, their presence around the table will be normalised and the quotas can be abandoned after providing a stepping stone to change.

Change is certainly required, as the statistics reflect, and there are still some significant barriers for women trying to join Australian boards. Monash University academics Kelly Tropea, Helen de Cieri and Cathy Sheehan examined the case for legislated quotas, outlined in *Quotas on Boards?*, and identified a series of formidable personal and structural barriers for Australian women. The personal barriers include lack of ambition for board seats, preference for family responsibilities, lack of CEO experience, lack of tenure, perceived skills deficit and a reluctance to nominate for roles. The structural barriers range from the macho Australian culture and lack of acceptance of women as leaders, male-dominated workplace cultures where long hours are expected, informal promotion policies, lack of transparency, and tokenism of women on boards. They concluded that quotas could lead to a backlash against appointing women, but advocated more transparency around board appointments and new obligations to interview at least two women for all board vacancies.

As their research shows, this topic has proved illuminating in unexpected ways and has revealed how strongly the main gender myths are still entrenched. A series of public debates and discussions have proved the point. In August 2010 I heard a spirited debate between Elizabeth Broderick, the Sex Discrimination Commissioner and David Gonski, Chancellor of UNSW, chair of ASX Ltd, Coca Cola Amatil Ltd and Investec Bank Australia Ltd on 'Board representation: Balancing the gender mix', hosted by the Sydney Institute. The discussion for (Broderick) and against (Gonski) introducing quotas started with common ground: both were in strong agreement that there were not enough women on boards. But views differed on how to address this scarcity, with Broderick advocating the introduction of 'temporary special measures', such as quotas, as a circuit breaker to speed up change and deliver a critical mass of at least 40 per cent women. She reminded the audience that there was a strong cultural connection with how women are treated in corporate life and in society.

On the other hand, Gonski argued that quotas compromise the ability of a business to operate as it sees fit and those laggard organisations that are not across this gender balance issue will fail anyway as 'they are not in tune with what is going on, they are not great businesses'. He warned that intervention to bolster the number of women could open up the floodgates for further measures and greater scrutiny. Boards should be able to invite women to join on their own terms, he added. It would be fair to say this comment did not go down well with the audience comprised mainly of women, nor did the unspecified warning about the repercussions of quotas and the assessment that women do not understand what will be unleashed. It's not the only time this has been presented as a reason to dismiss quotas.

'I do hope we do not go to quotas and believe it very strongly because I don't think those who advocate quotas know where it goes,' Gonski told a 2010 CEDA panel discussion called 'Women in leadership'. Quotas could mean women were token board appointments rather than earning jobs in their own right, he added. It was odd to hear this because moments earlier he had outlined in no uncertain terms why he believed there were plenty of talented women available to join boards, and that the men running Australian businesses were to blame for our poor track record in appointing women to boards. He said, 'I blame myself and many other of the men I know. It's not right and I can't understand why.'

According to Gonski, when he asked colleagues about the low level of women on boards many did indeed tell him there are not enough senior or experienced women to appoint, or that women would not fit in – or even that the bad language in the boardroom might upset women. 'All of these excuses sound extremely bad, and they are, and they are not acceptable.' He spelt out why the 'lack of women' argument was so hollow: for example, the concept that chief executive experience was a prerequisite for a board position was incorrect and that a board full of CEOs would be a nightmare, reminding the audience that he had never been a CEO. While it was important that directors fitted in with the board, that didn't mean they had to all be the same.

These debates certainly flesh out the drawbacks to both quotas and targets, which have to be considered to avoid a backlash. Even supporters of quotas are well aware these mechanisms can help as part of a range of measures and are a means to an end, not a complete solution. As I mentioned, targets are not without their critics either, who see plenty of problems with reaching some of the more ambitious goals. I spoke to ANZ executive and a member of the bank's diversity council, Nigel Williams, about this and he told me that like all targets you need to look at how the figure is calculated and not take the number at face value. 'The easiest way to meet them is to poach (senior women) off competitors or customers. It's more important to build talent and identify high performers and move them around,' he said. The real goal is actually about making gender equity measures part of standard business practices, not a band-aid measure or quick fix, and targets need to be part of a set of changes if they are to succeed.

Many women hold the same reservations about targets as they do for quotas, because they are already made to feel they have to justify their right to sit at the management table and hate the thought that they could be called a token appointment or haven't earned their job. There is also concern that targets for women in management depend on how you define management. Some sceptics quipped that job titles could well be changing for a lot of women to help reach targets and, of course, the scope and responsibility of a management role in one organisation can be very different in another.

The quota debate usually involves some reference to what is happening internationally too – and that's because quite a lot of countries are considering legislated quotas. In particular, the Norwegian experience of introducing legislated quotas for women on boards invariably makes its way into the conversation and is worth some attention, if only to help understand that the fear of dangerous precedents may be exaggerated. Yes, it is true Norway is a very small economy in Scandinavia with many glaring social and economic differences to Australia, but it was only when I interviewed Arne Hole, the Norewgian minister for equality and one of the architects of the legislation, that some of the context for the move became clearer.

The business community in Norway had a historically poor record with getting women onto boards

– about 6 per cent of directorships in 2002 were held by women before the legislation – while now there are close to 40 per cent women, Hole explained to me. It was actually a conservative government minister who decided enough was enough and introduced voluntary regulation to try and boost the level, but after three years the percentage remained stubbornly low. It was at this point the debate kicked up a notch or two. Norwegian business leaders warned of dire consequences if the legislation went ahead, even threatening to move their headquarters to other countries. Despite the outcry the law was eventually changed and while it's not perfect the effect has been dramatic with some positive and negative outcomes.

There are some women in Norway holding multiple board seats, but Hole quickly pointed out there are still many more men holding higher numbers of directorships than women. Unfortunately the statistical data doesn't show much improvement in the number of women in corporate leadership, despite the change around the board table. But the predicted economic ruin did not eventuate, with a number of leading business figures happy to concede that their main concerns were unfounded. Worries about a lack of qualified women for the roles were largely proved to be wrong as well. It became clear during our conversation that Hole regarded quotas as a circuit breaker for change and not a long-term necessity. The aim was really to get to a point where this kind of legislation was unnecessary, she said, and while forcing change is never ideal, sometimes there was no choice.

Australia's response to the quota debate has reflected its cultural position somewhere between the voluntary action favoured by the United States and the European path of either introducing or considering mandatory quotas. A number of EU countries, including France and Spain, are moving towards legislation to help lift women's representation on boards, which is often dubbed the 'Norwegian effect'. And interest has been growing in the EU. In July 2011 the European Parliament called for EU-wide legislation to ensure female directors make up at least 40 per cent of supervisory boards by 2020. This is not to say the path to legislated quotas in the EU is guaranteed. Many countries are not fans of such moves, with similar reactions from some business communities to those in Australia.

Viviane Reding, European Commission vice-president in charge of gender equality, has said that if voluntary action doesn't make much difference to the poor progress in most European countries then a 'targeted legal instrument' for the EU may be needed. In 2011 EU markets commissioner Michel Barnier indicated he was 'open to the idea' of official targets. 'The presence of women in the leadership of a country or a region or a business is a question of good governance for me,' he said in early 2011. His comments followed a widely reported faux pas by Deutsche Bank chief executive Josef Ackermann, who observed during a debate that appointing women to the bank's executive board would make it 'prettier and more colourful'. Oops.

Germany's Merkel government has veered away from introducing legislated quotas to date; however, some German companies have set targets of their own. In 2010 Deutsche Telekom, the country's sixth-biggest company with 260 000 staff, introduced targets for women in management, in a move similar to subsequent actions by the Commonwealth Bank, Westpac, Telstra and the federal Treasury. DT's management board, which is solely male, imposed a target of 30 per cent women managers by 2015, up from 13 per cent at the time. The company said the target was also part of its contracts with headhunters and expected to affect roughly 10 000 jobs.

In Britain, a report by former banker and government minister Mervyn Davies on why so few women are on British boards came out in early 2011. Davies had already indicated he was not convinced mandatory quotas were the right way to go. His suggestion was for FTSE 100-listed companies to set their own targets, with the veiled threat of government action if the status quo was not challenged within two years, which is more in line with Australia's new voluntary framework for reporting on diversity. Late in 2010 a group of British chairs and organisations set up The 30% Club, a body dedicated to boosting women's representation in the senior ranks of British businesses (30 per cent is considered the threshold needed to establish an influential critical mass).

In the United States the statistics on women in boardrooms show little change in the past few years, with women making up only 16 per cent of directors of Fortune 500 companies in 2011. Commentary there is also now focusing on the moves to quotas in some parts of the world, although the emphasis continues to be on voluntary schemes rather than formal goals. This lack of appetite for quotas may well be partly a legacy of the US Affirmative Action debates of the 1980s, which centred on hiring policies and college admissions systems that gave preference and/or additional weight to women and minorities.

Many believe there was a backlash from these measures. When US management guru Tom Peters visited Australia in 2011 he told a corporate audience that affirmative action quotas in the United States had served their purpose. But these days he's not a fan of the idea of imposing quotas for gender and he hoped they would not be needed to address gender inequity in business. However, the failure to target the women's market and boost management representation 'utterly infuriated' him. He stressed that it was not a question of personal beliefs about social justice but the sheer economic advantages that were being ignored.

The business case for better gender equity on boards and in management is backed by evidence from research around the world, although the data are often ignored in the clash about quotas. Numerous studies from Australia and internationally show a correlation between more women on boards and better bottom-line performance. The Reibey Institute, an Australian not-for-profit research centre, released analysis in 2011 showing that over the past three- and five-year periods, ASX500 companies with women directors on their boards delivered significantly higher return on equity (ROE) than those without women directors. There was an 8.7 per cent difference over five years and 6.7 per cent over three years.

So we know we have a problem with so few women on boards and in management (which seems to exist in most parts of the developed world); we know some of the causes and the likely consequences of doing nothing, but debate still rages about the best solutions when regulation is proposed. In fact, the popularity of targets in business is actually because most other options have been tried and haven't delivered.

One of the more popular avenues so far in Australia is the ubiquitous mentoring program, where a senior executive is matched with an aspiring woman to show her the ropes. A number of these have been launched by business lobby groups that have belatedly started to focus on low levels of women on boards, including the Australian Institute of Company Directors (this is really a case of better late than never). Industry group Women in Banking and Finance runs an annual mentoring program for women and the Business Council of Australia has its C-suite mentoring program. Women on Boards also runs a mentoring and professional development program.

Gaining insights from board veterans makes sense and in theory sounds like a reasonable idea. But given the male-dominated ranks on boards this means mentoring typically matches senior executive men with up-and-coming women, which is a classic paternal relationship and threatens to simply perpetuate the existing model. Certainly, if this is about understanding how the old boy's club works, then men are well placed to do it. But even in Australia there are more than a couple of women business leaders who could help to pass on their hard-won knowledge about navigating the barriers and getting on to boards. Word around the traps when these programs were being set up was that some very senior women were approached about these schemes, but, to their astonishment, were asked if they would like to be mentored rather than be a mentor.

The lack of women mentors doesn't send a particularly encouraging message to high-achieving women.

More than one woman board director has told me she found the arrangement insulting and patronising. The structure of these programs is something I believe needs more scrutiny (see myth 1).

In fact, a closer look reveals that both the Australian Institute of Company Directors and the Business Council of Australia were targeting 'board-ready' and 'high-achieving' women for these programs. Why would high-achieving or board-ready women need special attention? Surely they already have the skills and expertise to be legitimate candidates for boards or executive roles anyway? Shouldn't the attention be on the existing boards and their old-fashioned attitudes to women? It seems the mentoring relationship may actually be mostly about developing the informal networks that remain off-limits to women, but continue to be prerequisites for a directorship. If so, some concrete measures to ensure more transparency around board vacancies and the appointment process would also be very helpful. This was a recommendation of the CAMAC's *Diversity on Boards of Directors* report, released in 2009. While stopping short of recommending quotas for women on boards it stressed that success in addressing the lack of women depended on corporate leaders and shareholders understanding the need for more transparency.

Meanwhile, as noted, the number of women appointed to ASX200 boards has increased to nearly

14 per cent in Australia (at March 2012). Of course, there's still a long way to go – there are 64 companies on the ASX200 that do not have any women at all on their boards. The women directors appointed are all exceptional people, although most of them, like many male directors, have years of board experience and a number of directorships already. The other note of caution about these mentoring programs and the current efforts to boost the number of women is to ensure the boy's club is not duplicated with women. But it is a marvellous example of how a bit of concentration on the matter managed to trigger some action and revealed the appropriate women candidates who can't have been so hard to find after all. Mentoring certainly achieves one result – mentors become aware of the array of well-qualified women who could take up board roles. In fact, some mentors apparently become quite competitive about getting 'their' woman a directorship.

When some thought has been put into the design of mentoring programs they can be a valuable tool and not a one-way process. The men involved as mentors can learn a lot from the process too. Former BHP chair Don Argus, who is an AICD mentor, told a conference in 2009 that he was quite astonished at the calibre of the mentorees, which may tell us more about the lack of women he has encountered than the quality of those women being mentored. No matter, at least he got the message. The flurry of mentoring programs has managed to trigger some action and revealed a broader group of women candidates. But to make mentoring truly effective there needs to be a parallel effort to open up the pathways to the boardroom for all.

While there have been some moves in this direction, the barriers remain stubbornly in place in many companies and some male directors are well aware of that. For all the recent progress, the core problems around gender equity in senior ranks of business and boards are hardly new and were much the same 20 years ago, as former NSW premier and businessman Nick Greiner told an AICD forum in Sydney in mid-2011. Along with a clutch of company chairs, Greiner was at the launch of the 2011 AICD mentoring scheme. A couple of directors at the same function were upbeat about the future, but some, such as Insurance Australia Group chair Brian Schwartz, warned that progress cannot be guaranteed without vigilance and continued effort, and Woolworths chair James Strong made the point that the supply of women for boards is contingent upon increasing the number of women in management.

Let's be honest, the reason these efforts have been made was not because a group of powerful men woke up one morning and decided to share the power more equitably. It struck me at the time that if the momentum was to continue it would help to be realistic about what really triggered some action after decades of neglect. In short, it comes down to two main factors: consistent data and the threat of regulation. Some of the momentum for change is even starting to register in our most traditionally male bastions. When I attended a forum for women in oil and gas in 2011 I was not expecting to find support for targets or quotas, but Ann Pickard, Shell Australia's country chairwoman and a speaker at the event, said setting targets for women in senior jobs is necessary. And she's also a fan of putting quotas in place for women on boards.

'The gender mix in Australia's oil and gas sector is not good, and we have a long way to go,' she told a 2011 Perth forum, 'Women in Oil and Gas' (run by Ernst & Young and the Australian Petroleum Production and Exploration Association). The oil and gas sector may be a rapidly growing part of the economy with plenty of job opportunities, but it is facing a major struggle to boost the number of women it employs. Women make up only about 10 per cent of employees in the sector on average and about 18 per cent of the overall resources sector. Some of the problems for women working in oil and gas are peculiar to the sector as it is heavily male-dominated, many jobs are located in remote regions and professional roles often require qualifications women are less likely to hold.

'You can have a CEO saying something, but if you don't drive it through then there's no point,' Pickard said. When she started in her current role in 2010, Pickard had one woman reporting to her; by 2011 she had three. Graduate hiring was 50 per cent women, she said, and it was also important to be aware of subjective measures used in recruitment and promotion procedures. Sometimes the 'best qualified' person translated as part of the old boy's club, and this was particularly true of board appointments where who you know is often just as important as what you know. I think Pickard may also be finding that Perth in particular is a small town.

Sometimes you need a fresh perspective like Pickard's to refresh and revive a debate. As an American with many years international experience, her thoughts on quotas that day made a few people sit up and take notice, including Don Voelte, then CEO of Woodside, who said her views were changing his mind about quotas. Pickard was not on a bandwagon, but stated her belief that after many decades running businesses, progress for women would only come from changing the rules. Proposing a more structured approach to boosting women's presence on boards has definitely pushed the gender debate to a new level.

But what do other women think? I mentioned that some women bristle at the mention of quotas, but surveys show many have gradually warmed to the idea.

A 2009 study from Women on Boards (well before the 2011 increase in women directors was registered) confirmed that 50 per cent of female directors supported legislated gender quotas for public-listed company boards. Historically, female directors have been reluctant to advocate any form of regulation for boosting representation. Women in these roles, as I have mentioned, are generally highly sensitive to accusations of tokenism or suggestions they have taken advantage of their gender. But sometimes the sheer glacial speed of change converts them. A woman director on a listed company board once told me she had been opposed to quotas for these reasons, but started to reconsider when she realised that a number of informal quotas already operated. The board she joined was based in Sydney, but routinely made sure a director from Melbourne was appointed. She was a fan of the idea if all else failed to make a change, particularly after watching the 'jobs for the boys' system at work and the lack of real transparency in the process of appointing new directors. It seemed to her that being an old friend or colleague of a director still had more to do with getting a foot in the door than anything else.

At a roundtable discussion on gender in 2010, Robert Care, then chair of engineering firm Arup Australasia, also backed calls for more urgent formal action:

> It just seems to me that we've actually had
> quota systems for 150 years. We've had a lot of
> corporations in existence which have been about
> coming from the right school, from the right golf
> club, so actually the quotas are implicit. They're
> not defined. They're not explicit. If one were to
> move to a quota system, you would actually be
> merely balancing out the existing quota system.

The fact that so many female directors backed quotas reflected how bad the situation had become, and Claire Braund, executive director of Women on Boards, said the results indicated more women were becoming disillusioned that anything is going to change. 'They have spent their careers hearing that self-belief, application, merit, education and the pipe-line will deliver them positions at the top – only to find it is all a myth.'

Similar findings emerged from the *Women Getting into Boards* study in 2009, which contained inter-views with 317 women, mostly Australian, and 67 per cent with board experience. The majority believed the recruitment process of boards overall is inequita-ble as it lacks transparency, clearly defined and real-istic criteria, and is advertised to a selective group. Women do not have the opportunity to apply because they do not know which boards have vacancies, and when they do apply they are judged against criteria that are discriminatory and attitudes that rate their achievements and experiences as unimportant and un-transferable.

This is why the idea of quotas or targets to aim for in women's appointments should be considered, said Diann Rodgers-Healy, director of the Australian Centre for Leadership for Women.

> Government needs to step in and make boards accountable and pursue quotas. Obviously women (applying for board roles) want the experience, and once the opportunity comes through they do perform. It's not just about choice, it's about opportunity, and we do not have the opportunity.

While the spectre of board quotas has been a useful conversation starter, the fragmented and sometimes confusing debate has definitely left some commentators and observers fed up. They believe – with some justification – that too much attention has been paid to this issue at the expense of much more important and broader workplace gender barriers.

Although more women on boards is a welcome sign, there is a danger with too much preoccupation in this particular area, according to UK consultant Avivah Wittenberg-Cox, who runs a business advising companies about gender issues.

> The focus is quite a dangerous one – there's way too much focus on women on boards, which is a relatively insignificant issue and concerns a few dozen women when there are tens of thousands of women in organisations. I think it's a real shame; it was easy to get women on boards and that's why it's happened. That's throwing crumbs to the starving. We need to be a lot smarter. We have to stop fixing the women and trying to turn women into men. We have enough experience of gender balancing the world and some countries manage better.

China, Poland and Russia, for example, with their communist heritage, have made the significant rule changes to normalise dual income earning, she pointed out to me. The Anglo-Saxon capitalist model is far more of a challenge and will never accept legislated quotas for women because it goes against the grain.

I agree with Avivah's rationale that board composition and appointments can be changed relatively quickly and without rocking the boat too much. As has become apparent, no matter what the naysayers believe, there are actually plenty of appropriate women for directorships once you start to really look around. But I don't believe we should drop the efforts for better equity on boards in the belief that it hampers efforts to boost women in management. Both are pressing problems that can be simultaneously addressed.

I think the quota discussion will remain current for some time. An evidence-based look at quotas reveals they are not in themselves the danger that many business leaders seem to believe they are, and targets are rapidly spreading across the business world. I think there is some danger that the gains made on boards in recent years will be seen as mission accomplished and the attention will therefore dwindle. Pressure should be maintained on boards to open up their processes and for bodies like the AICD to look at a range of measures that include but are not restricted to mentoring schemes, which run the risk of reinforcing traditional gender roles and even replicating the old boy's club with a female version.

I'm not sure we will ever see legislated quotas in Australia, but I am sure that whenever I have deconstructed the main criticisms of such a move I have won a few converts to the idea that it would not be as devastating as some believe. But I've also come to understand that the negative perceptions about women directors appointed under a quota system seem as likely to cause problems, and even become self-fulfilling, as the reality. Acdemic psychologist Cordelia Fine commented in an article in *The Monthly*, 'Even if corporate Australia is exploding with women thoroughly deserving of senior leadership roles, if the dominant cultural mindset supposes otherwise then prescriptive forms of affirmative action may have undermining, self-fulfilling psychological effects'.

Angst about imposed change is nothing new and reflects understandable fear and resistance. The prestige involved in these roles has ensured that the door to the boardroom has barely opened, despite evidence about the benefits to business from a mix of directors. As corporate social responsibility expert Paul Klein asked in his *Forbes CSR* blog in 2011: 'If women are so important, why are the largest corporations shutting them out of the boardroom? I offer two primary reasons: not enough women have reached the C-suite level and many boardrooms remain rooted in a culture that perpetuates and rewards traditional male networks.' From that perspective a gender quota looks dangerous indeed to those already at the table.

But the conversation about board quotas actually helped give birth to the targets for women in management now spreading across our businesses. If they are effective, they will be the source of many more women contenders for the boardroom. It's hard to ignore the similarities in the frameworks for both, and as targets become part of business practice I suspect the objection to quotas on the grounds they are dangerous will start to recede. This alarmist reaction has been less about fears of a backlash on women and more about the objection to regulation and interference with a system that has been comfortable and unchallenged for many decades. Challenging the mythology about quotas is about confronting the entrenched defenders of an elite power system. That's what tackling all the myths is about, but the time for this particular puncturing is absolutely right.

CASE STUDY: WOOLWORTHS

Supermarket chain Woolworths, which employs 191 000 staff, is using innovative ways to attract and retain women employees through flexible work, job redesign and leave arrangements. Over the past few years it has introduced a number of measures to help, including paid maternity leave, retention strategies and a range of flexible work arrangements for the management ranks. HR director, Kim Schmidt, says Woolworths's motivation for transforming work practices was attracting and retaining skilled employees as the business grew.

'We had a lot of women in the business but when we looked at the senior level we didn't,' Schmidt says. 'The things we put in place were around flexibility and retaining women who were returning from maternity leave, and we started attracting more female talent into the business.'

These days men are also using flexible work arrangements. And Schmidt says it's clear to her that employees working on flexible hours are not only well organised, but often the most productive people.

> When are people most productive? When they are engaged. If you want to keep people engaged you need to be able to do it in a way that suits their lifestyle and expectations. It really has made a lot of difference and loosened up the culture a bit as people adapt and work differently.

The gender work at Woolworths, under Kim Schmidt and former CEO Michael Luscombe, has helped boost the number of women in management (up from 16.7 per cent in 2004 to 28 per cent in 2011). It has set a target of having 33 per cent of women in the three senior levels of management, including the board, by 2015. Woolworths also uses a variety of data and metrics to keep track of the pay and promotion of women. Luscombe said actions speak louder than words.

> When you actually do something – you do promote someone while they're on maternity leave, or people do come back in senior positions and they do work three days a week or work Tuesday to Saturday or they do a job share – it's very visible. You don't send out a memo. People just see it and go OK, so this is all right.

He said it was important for women to 'shine' in areas of the business considered to be male-dominated or male-only positions. Julie Coates, who runs the Big W stores, for example, went into the logistics division at one stage, and appointing female distribution centre managers also sent a very big signal to everybody that trucks and warehouses are not male domains. Luscombe went on to say:

> They are the domains of smart people and good people leaders. There are a whole host of other things – making sure that in our succession planning we have both male and female participants in the senior decisions and the field that's considered has an equal sprinkling of men and women depending on what's available. Likewise, since our refloat in '93 always we've had at least one female board member – presently we have two.

Woolworths makes a particular effort to measure the gender split in the business, too. Luscombe said the organisation actually measures what female representation is at the various levels of the business and actively makes sure pay levels are as identical as possible, having regard to relative experience. According to Schmidt:

> Our customers mainly are female, and if you get diversity around the table and in thinking, you get

better outcomes for business and customers. It's the next level of the conversation: the benefits diversity brings to customers and the community, and the synergy we get from that.

MYTH 6:
WOMEN SHOULD ACT MORE LIKE MEN (AND THEY ARE THEIR OWN WORST ENEMIES)

A few years ago I was at a Women on Boards conference listening to a panel discussion on why women struggled to get ahead as fast as their male peers in the workforce. One of the topics discussed was the apparent failure of women to successfully conduct pay negotiations and the need for them to lift their game. It's a favourite theme in these kinds of conversations and has been dubbed the deficit model or remedial approach to women (see myth 2). One of the panellists – a distinguished businessman – said he was a bit tired of hearing about this assumption. Yes, he said, his male employees did tend to be more assertive when asking for a pay rise and while the women who worked for him also asked him for pay increases, they did so less often and asked for less. Anyway, he said, it was his belief that women shouldn't be urged to behave more like the aggressive men in this case, but for men to behave a bit more like the women.

It was a nice flip around of the pat advice handed out to women and packaged up in books and seminars as a matter of course over recent times. For decades women have been told one of the main reasons for a lack of gender equity is their faulty behaviour – too nice, too quiet, too emotional, too bitchy. Too, well, female. And the solution? Toughen up and act like the blokes. There's been an avalanche of advice along these lines to 'remedy' this sad situation, ranging from exhortations to be more assertive and ask for promotions more often, wear certain clothes to work, never cry, and even to avoid red lipstick in the office or risk being mistaken for a pole dancer. Seriously. And so it goes on.

Sometimes academic research about the biases against females and how merit judgements are shaped by implicit preconceptions about gender can end up in some pretty absurd advice too, according to academic and author Cordelia Fine in 'Status quota'. Researchers reviewing bias in evaluations of candidates for traditionally masculine roles, published in the journal *Academic Medicine*, recommended women douse themselves in masculine scent and make sure they conceal pregnancy. These tips 'reflect research showing that femininity triggers less generous assessments of ability'. No surprise then that advice on how to turn into a replica of a man could seem a possible solution.

The neat packaging of lists for women with an emphasis on learning how to be more 'professional' or male-like has certainly struck a chord and it's a very appealing format. When I reviewed the best seller *Nice Girls Just Don't Get It* by Lois Frankel and Carol Frohlinger, I pointed out what a hugely successful example of the genre this book is – the fifth along these lines written or co-authored by Frankel. In this instalment the authors argue that the poor treatment of women in the workplace goes back to how most women are socialised from childhood as 'nice girls' who put others' needs before their own. The proposition is clearly enormously attractive to many women who wonder why all their effort and study has left them worse off than their male peers, but a list of self-help tips is dangerous. Women drawn to this format are told to get their act together, discard their socialising, follow some rules and, bingo, the barriers will begin to disappear.

Unfortunately, this is mostly delusional. There's no real leeway in this scenario for the gender bias built into most institutions, the power structures that continue to favour a dominant group (mostly middle-aged white men) and the growing evidence that double standards apply from the moment a woman walks into an office, regardless of her skills, childhood experience or behaviour. To be fair, some of the book's advice does have tactical value, but much of it could easily be applied to men with less dominant personalities. There's no point in giving women tips on how to dress and lower their voices if there is a failure to even challenge the idea that this is all about reflecting the existing norms of male-dominated workplaces. Even if the 'nice girls' theory is valid for some women, what about the many who already practise the compliant strategies advocated by the book? Why aren't they running the team or even the corporation? Plenty of women – I know many, including myself – are well aware that acquiescence and martyrdom are unhelpful, yet they have not fared better in the world of paid work than the so-called 'nice girls'.

I also worry that this kind of approach risks burdening women once again with debilitating concerns about not being good enough. These kinds of admonishments to get with the program can prove to be a distraction from understanding the real causes of gender discrimination. Telling women it's mostly their – or their parents' – fault and that they can change their destiny by modifying behaviour, is misleading at best. Of course, there's no evidence that any of this advice has made the slightest difference to women's progress or workplace equity. In fact, you'd have to conclude that either the scores of women buying these kinds of books are not actually applying the tips, or if they are it's been unsuccessful because there's been little change to the statistics on women's representation in the workforce, particularly in those top tiers. It has, however, probably further demoralised a fair few women who understandably feel that their gender is once again THE problem, and requires justification.

As I have already argued about the meritocracy myth, the broader problem with advising women to act more like men in the workplace or suffer the consequences hinges on some faulty premises. The problems women often encounter are not due to how each woman behaves nor the success or failure of their individual efforts, but the fact that they are female and what that signifies. This is where the anecdotal evidence reinforced by stereotyping comes in, which is unlikely to be erased by a few stop-gap modifications. Tackling these problems via remedial tips also assumes that every workplace is a well-oiled machine where human relations run by the book and scrupulous fairness guides all decisions. Even the most loyal corporate citizens find that a bit rich.

The real problem with this myth, like meritocracy, is that it also reinforces the status quo. When you believe that the solution to gender inequity is about changing those pesky women there's a perfect excuse to do nothing to alter the way the system works, from recruitment to training to promotions. It gives very little – or no – attention to the role that a hostile workplace plays for women, no matter how they behave or the colour of their lipstick. It ignores the increasingly well-documented reality that the way to survive and get ahead in most businesses is based on a fairly limited suite of behaviours associated with a certain kind of male style (which doesn't even apply to many men). Neither is there much attention paid to the growing evidence that what appears to work well for ambitious men going up the ladder can have a very different outcome for women who mimic such behaviour.

As always, I love a good bit of research to provide some perspective in these areas. In myth 3 I mentioned the Catalyst study of 2011, *The Myth of the Ideal Worker,* where it was argued that the idea women fail to put their hat in the ring for promotions and career steps needs reassessing. Results from the survey found that doing all the right things to get ahead worked well for men but did not provide as great an advantage for women. Basically, behaving like men simply didn't meet with the same response or results for women, and the researchers concluded that women needed to adopt different strategies from men, rather than imitate them.

The rules are different for men and women – and behaviour is viewed very differently too. Plenty of well-qualified women know exactly what constitutes the formal and informal codes for getting ahead, so to assume they never ask for or seek opportunities defies commonsense. Attributing their failure to climb the ladder to behaving like a woman is not exactly confidence-inducing. Many studies on workplace behaviour and gender have also found that women who are deemed to behave in unfeminine ways or are seen as aggressive are penalised for their behaviour. What's good for the gander is not so good for the goose.

Thankfully, some attention is also being paid to the other part of this equation – the assumption that there is indeed a uniform successful 'male' way of behaving and negotiating the workplace. When the gender lens turns to men instead of women in the workplace some light is usually shed. Instead of concentrating on why women fail to progress, a bit of research on men's attitudes to areas considered 'female only' reveals more similarities than differences. Men and women say they want to devote significant time to their family life, and in their careers both groups also have remarkably similar goals, according to Australian research in 2011, *What Men Want* by The 100% Project.

This shouldn't really come as a surprise. However, in such a fraught area of debate there has been far too much reliance on the anecdotes that ramp up differences rather than evidence to the contrary. One research report, of course, does not represent a sea change. But a different perspective does help to remind us that the perennial issues that emerge when this topic is discussed are almost always considered to be the responsibility of women, who are required to adjust to the existing system. Change that premise and the picture starts to look different – as does the group keen to take part in the discussion.

At a forum on The 100% Project findings, which I attended in Melbourne, the audience consisted of far more men than would usually turn up to events of this kind, who asked many of the questions about the study. Most were actively interested in the debate and had quite personal comments to make about their own family situation. When you take a moment to recognise that more and more men are taking a different view of their caring and domestic roles these days, it can help move this debate away from the deficit idea. It also makes our organisational practices look distinctly out of tune with social norms. And it challenges the idea that women are always the best nurturers and carers, which often feeds the assumption they therefore somehow lack the necessary skills to be effective in paid work.

About 75 per cent of Australian men surveyed (430 respondents, 43 per cent male, employed across sectors, but with the majority working in financial and professional services) for *What Men Want* expected to devote a significant amount of time to rearing their children. Whether they end up devoting this time or not is another question. I have some doubt about the realistic expectations some people have about caring work, particularly when they may never have spent time looking after small children on their own or doing the bulk of the thankless household chores. However, the results also show that 39 per cent of men had asked for greater work/life balance at some point in their career, but only 7 per cent of men were in part-time roles compared to 25 per cent of women. So it seems these requests from men may have been for temporary measures, perhaps for special circumstances, rather than long-term changes to work patterns. The main reason men gave in the research for not asking for more workplace flexibility was a belief that such a request would damage their careers.

However, when asked about their commitment to their career, women and men had very similar responses. In fact, slightly more women (25 per cent) agreed with the statement 'I value being involved in a career and expect to devote time and energy to developing it' than men (22 per cent). Chair of The 100% Project, Frances Feenstra, is a former professional services executive and a passionate believer in better gender equity, and says the aim of the group is to see all of Australia's leadership talent contributing to our social and economic future. This research backs up the proposition that some of the main structural inhibitors for women are also bad news for men, so it's not as though female behaviour is the problem here but the inflexible structures many people work within.

The deficit model is a reminder that women are viewed in a very different light to male employees, even after so many years of analysis about gender in the workplace. When it comes to women in the limelight there is a distinct and onerous level of attention paid to their gender and failure to conform to male leadership models rather than their expertise or experience (see myth 3). Unfortunately, there are few signs of this changing, and I was particularly struck by the coverage of Christine Lagarde's ascension to the top job at the International Monetary Fund in 2011. In a way this coverage shows us that women in leadership must overcome the deficit model and then some. They almost have to be super-human and sexy with it. And when they are seen as failing, or not successfully walking the fine line between femininity and authority, they risk getting torn to pieces. Lagarde's predecessor, Dominique Strauss-Kahn, resigned in mid-2011 after being charged with sexual assault in New York (the charges were eventually dropped). Lagarde, formerly the French finance minister, launched a campaign for the IMF job that attracted plenty of interest and, of course, there's been plenty of media focus and profiles since she stepped into this influential and high-profile position.

The fact that Lagarde is very experienced and

highly qualified for her job seems not to be in question, although the appointment bears some of the hallmarks of the so-called 'glass cliff' theory (see myth 2). This is the idea that a disproportionate number of women in leadership jobs are appointed at a time of crisis in an organisation, possibly because they are regarded as a last resort or a safer bet, or fewer male contenders are willing to put their hands up at such a risky time. Regardless of why these appointments are made, women coming into power in this way typically face enormous challenges and so usually don't last long in the role. That seems an unlikely outcome for Lagarde. However, media coverage since she became one of the world's most powerful women has highlighted her looks and style as much as her credentials. Having had the fortune to interview Lagarde a few years ago, I can certainly confirm she is a remarkable and impressive woman with plenty of presence. But do we really need to run a profile of one of the world's leading finance specialists with the headline 'Is this the world's sexiest woman?'. Would a profile of a handsome French man have earned a similar headline? The descriptions of her clothes and looks have bordered on excessive, particularly when compared with similar profiles of men. And there's been a tendency for admiring descriptions of her enduring femininity – with a distinct sense of relief that the road to the top hasn't meant giving up her womanliness.

Phew. This is one tricky balancing act. No wonder women in leadership roles say it's an extra tough gig for them.

Navigating through such distinct gender judgements about ability and style supports the classic cliché that women are really inherently different in many respects to men. No wonder we are told women particularly need help with these toxic workplace dynamics – it's a bloke thing and women will struggle to understand it, even if they drink the Kool Aid and start pretending to be men. I've never had time for the men are from Mars and women are from Venus proposition, whether at work or not. Of course, women are socialised differently, as noted by the Lois Frankels of this world. A battery of books have also been written about male and female brains, the vast structural differences in how we think and the size of certain lobes. Many have concluded that women are inferior in some key ways to men, which turn out to be particularly pertinent to success in paid work. What a surprise.

But are we really biologically fundamentally poles apart? Thankfully a refutation of this whole genre has been surfacing over the last couple of years, which is very welcome and refreshing. It's great for those moments when someone blithely claims women are really another species and the sexes will never understand each other (imagine using race instead of gender in that context and the generalisations do sound rather ridiculous). However, there are several signs that the fervour for a biological determinist explanation of gender differences is finally starting to fade after years of hearing that women's hormones make them more emotional and intuitive, and less logical.

The biological rationale has been a handy fallback in debates about the poor representation of women in the areas of science and maths, and in the ranks of the powerful. It strikes me as highly convenient and just a bit suspicious to find a scientific cause for this poor representation as women finally start to really compete for high-status jobs and power. Many of the more serious efforts quote research and up-to-the-minute neuroscience for their conclusions, which in recent years have been critically examined by a group of feminist biologists and researchers.

For those who have always found such determinist explanations dodgy, to say the least, the rise in counter-arguments is very welcome. One such critique is *Brain Storm: The Flaws in the Science of Sex Differences* by Rebecca Jordan-Young. It was only when reading a review of this book that the reason for the wave of rebuttals became clearer to me. Feminist sociologist Hilary Rose and neuroscientist Steven Rose, in their *London Review of Books* review of *Brain Storm*, pointed out that it has taken a while to get some opposing views on 'the female brain' theory because the forces that prevented women from studying science also prevented them from researching their own scientific arguments. It was only in the 1970s, they wrote, that feminist biologists started to build up a head of steam, particularly after the publication of E O Wilson's *Sociobiology*, which claimed that genes rather than environment played the key role in determining behaviour, thus entrenching women's subservient position. In her research for *Brain Storm*, Jordan-Young discovered 'a hodgepodge of tiny samples, inadequate controls and extravagant conclusions'.

The revelation that much of the research in this area was flawed or invalid was also highlighted by Australian academic Cordelia Fine. She too contends that context and preconceptions have a major bearing on how these studies are conducted and reported. Turns out environment and bias have a lot of bearing in what is studied in the first place. As the review of Jordan-Young's book points out, researchers' essentialist preconceptions lead them to ignore context, above all the fact that gender identities do not spring fully formed from the genome or from the organisation of the newborn infant's brain.

Despite all the changes in male and female roles in western societies at work and home, we still seek traditional reference points and terms when we think or interact with each other, according to another Australian author to tackle this topic Jane McCredie in *Making Boys and Girls*.

> We learn them early, integrate them into our identities, charge them with extra energy as we become sexual beings, defining ourselves by them even when we resist them. Faced with the unsettling fluidity of much of modern life, some of us have retreated, seeking comfort in old certainties about the essential natures of men and women.

Yet, she points out, it is the constant interaction between biology and environment that helps construct who we are. Perhaps the popularity of biological-based sexism is about the comfort factor. To attribute the continuing gender discrimination in society to an inflexible, inherited brain structure that makes women unfit for leadership, for example, could come as a relief to some.

The mythology about the supposed science of gender brain differences really gained momentum in the last few years, but, according to Fine, in reality the gender differences in brain structure are minor and there is virtually no scientific evidence at all that brain structure has a direct effect on the way our minds function. At heart, it's a classic nature-versus-nurture debate at a time when many of us have

become preoccupied with nature. This may explain
the eagerness with which men and women seem to
greet the concept that biological difference under-
lies the supposed preference men have for maths and
women for humanities, or pink for girls and blue for
boys, a constructed preference if ever there was one.
As Fine points out, until the mid-20th century the
colour coding was actually the other way around.

But this ramping up of the case for innate differences between men and women has some distinctly
serious consequences for the workplace, where the
struggle for gender equity has faltered. Neuroscience
has all the trappings of science and it is being used
to feed old gender stereotypes, says Fine, a visiting
scholar at the Melbourne Business School.

> There are books, to target business leaders, in
> this category which are suggesting organisational
> applications and things business leaders can do
> that are misleading and about old stereotypes.
> Initially the idea [for my book] was to say 'this
> popular work is misusing the data and let's
> remember socialisation'. Let's see what science
> shows us about gender. It wasn't only that books
> were misusing the results, but close up, it was full
> of holes. It's been given a very popular spin …
> it says 'please pander to all the stereotypes and
> navigate them as best you can'.

Originally, Fine's curiosity about the science of gender differences was also piqued by having her own children.

> It's really about personal experience. As an interested parent ... I read *Why Gender Matters* [by Leonard Sax] and it was about why we should educate girls differently and I found it interesting and looked up the statistics and was really shocked at how unscientific the data was. I started to get interested in how neuroscience was being used in popular books about gender and I decided to confirm it.

The more she looked into the topic, the more Fine was askance. Many of the studies quoted with great authority in popular texts are simply inaccurate or based on small studies with minor discrepancies between the sexes. Or they fail to take into account the impact that context, assumptions and stereotypes have on women's behaviour and performance – the effect known as stereotype threat. This is what happens, for example, when you tell a group of women they will have difficulty completing a maths test. Bingo, when they sit for the test even those with good mathematical skills perform less competently.

It's a new way of recycling women's 'special' way

of thinking and it is positively crazy for people to think in black-and-white stereotypes. We should value empathy, but it's a slippery slope to see these as female things. They come as a package – that men are thinkers and women are feelers – and it hasn't served women well. They serve women very badly in the workplace and they suffer as a result of it and they are not based on science.

Part of the deal with promoting these ideas is the promise of simple solutions to complex problems, she adds. The offer is 'you buy one book and training package and you will increase diversity in your work-place'. But it doesn't actually work that way. The workplace problems are more complex.

> They can feel intractable and women are dealing with the second shift at home, there's income discrimination – which in one instance will be small but over a career will accumulate – and it becomes discrimination based on these stereotypes. So these books are dressing up the solutions with neuroscience. It appalled me that these books, which have no scientific validity, are being embraced by corporates.

As to addressing workplace problems, she says,

there's no silver bullet. She can't see any simple solutions because these things are mentally reinforcing and can't be addressed at any one level. In the minds of individuals, in the community and in the whole social structure of the environment, inequality feeds into people's minds – if you only target one level it will probably not work.

For organisations the best approach may be awareness of these issues and changing or vetting recruitment practices and criteria for jobs to avoid bias, including associating certain 'male' skills with leadership roles. But many people find these ideas plausible, Fine says, because they tap into well-established norms about what men and women are like. The rise of neurosexism, as she dubbed it, also reflects a recent preoccupation with genetics, DNA and hormones.

Fine says social science experiments show people aren't aware of how stereotypes are influencing their judgement, and the majority of people think they are not biased. Neuroscience makes us complacent about existing inequality and less confident, and it undermines men and women.

The deficit model that links women's failure in the workplace to special feminine qualities that are not appreciated or valued takes on a much nastier tone when classic human failings are classified as particularly female. I've added another myth to the idea that women are always in need of a makeover in the workplace. While they are perceived to lack the necessary skills because of their gender, there's also quite a strong belief that women have way too much bitchiness and a propensity for back-stabbing that holds their entire gender back. When you combine these assumptions it seems to leave little room to manoeuvre: women don't have what it takes and what they do have is a hindrance. Our sex thus becomes a double handicap, which once again diverts attention from both the structures we work in and those holding power in the workplace.

It's amazing how tenacious these presumptions about female-only transgressions have become. Women are their own worst enemies, I have been told on a regular basis by a wide range of women, who usually nod sagely as they deliver this statement. It's as though they have cracked the answer and it was something we all should have expected. It depresses me on a few levels, because it has become clearer to me that the strong message about problems women encounter being all their own fault is obviously hitting home. And it also worries me because many women are actually using this expression as shorthand to describe how women behave poorly at work – just like men – and thus stymie their female colleagues. That's a serious misreading of power relations.

It's revealing to read what women say they feel about other women in the workplace, a topic discussed in a series of round table discussions held by CEDA in their 2010–11 Women in Leadership forums around Australia. Some of the comments, which are similar to those I often hear, include: 'I can sometimes be fearful of women who are manipulative and yet men who behave the same are not deemed manipulative, they are deemed as influencers. Why is this so?'; 'There is unconscious behaviour in organisations; it's rife, an underlying anger towards other successful women. Women are really angry with other women and they don't like that female authority'; 'As a minority in a competitive culture, women are often pitted against each other. It's natural to want to be the best woman in the room. However, this engenders competition'; 'There is no support from our own sisterhood; basically women are criticising women.'

I know women behave badly at times, because I do, and I know plenty of women just like me. We are human after all, not saints, and as I often remind the audiences I speak to about this, men also behave very badly at work to each other and to women. We don't call them special names for this – ball breaker, ladder-puller – because that's what we expect from men in the rough-and-tumble world of work. 'Ladder-puller' is only applied to those ghastly women who reach senior jobs and pull the ladder up after them by not helping other women get ahead. There is no term for the legions of men who also behave like this – possibly many more than women – as men are often condoned and even rewarded for self-promoting and aggressive ambition.

When I looked into the ladder-pulling phenomena I found a variety of views on why this idea is so pervasive and whether or not it actually holds true. Jayne Hrdlicka, an executive at Qantas and board director, explained that she had once thought it was unnecessary to go out of her way to mentor other women or support women's networks.

> Sometimes the price of success in a male-
> dominated team is modifying your behaviour
> so you don't stand out. You feel you could get
> criticised for pulling other women up. I went
> through a stage in my career where I thought
> I'm no different. Then I thought, I've had unique
> success but I don't want to draw attention to it.

While a partner at consulting firm Bain, Hrdlicka initially thought setting up a network for women was not needed, but then changed her mind. She observed that most successful women have gone through that kind of epiphany because they realise that if every woman had to go through what they did to get ahead there will never be many women at the top. Some women in senior jobs are particularly sensitive to being seen as a token woman and go out of their way to avoid being seen as female-friendly.

Board director and former CEO, Gordon Cairns, told me that he didn't believe senior women were less helpful to other women, but their very high calibre means they perhaps become blind to the struggles of others. 'The exceptional women who make it because they are exceptional believe that it's Darwinian – and because they have made it maybe they don't feel that the situation for other women is as tough as it is made out.' While this doesn't mean they punish other women, it can make them less sympathetic to the problems facing less senior women or reluctant to be seen as the standard bearer for the gender.

When the bar is set so high for women and they either don't comply with the deficit advice or alternatively take unusually courageous steps to defend themselves and call sexist or bad behaviour there are usually strong penalties – and criticism can come from unexpected quarters. As an example of the complexity of this discussion you can't go past the fallout when young publicist Kristy Fraser-Kirk made sexual harassment claims against David Jones CEO Mark McInnes in 2010. He resigned from his high-profile job and actually acknowledged he had not behaved as he should have – so unlike other such claims there was no suggestion the victim had made it all up or had an axe to grind.

To launch a formal complaint about sexual harassment is not for the faint-hearted, and much of the reaction was unedifying and some unexpected. It was probably years of anti-bullying and sexual harassment awareness that helped give Fraser-Kirk the knowledge of her rights and the courage to act, although in practice her complaint was condemned by some as an overreaction. Formally, most business executives condemned McInnes's behaviour, but informally there were plenty who believed he was simply unlucky to get caught. The incident was certainly a hot topic of discussion in many boardrooms, but some women directors told me the discussion around the table was less concerned with sorting out a decent system to prevent such behaviour and more about how to make a nuisance factor go away. Nonetheless, a range of senior business women and some men told me how disgusted they were with the way Fraser-Kirk was portrayed during the incident.

The publicity campaign surrounding the case revealed that smearing the victim is still a popular tool – and unfortunately, that message fell on fertile ground. Surprisingly, a number of women who worked with Fraser-Kirk told journalists she should have just shut up and put up with McInnes's behaviour, which was a well-known pattern within the retailer. While not excusing such callousness, I think in these cases women reflect back the norms of the workplace and those in power, and in this much-reported incident there was a closing of the ranks among employees from loyalty and fear, and a tendency to find fault with a relatively junior employee who upset the apple cart. Sadly, it's not unusual. The DJs case revealed a concerted and cynical campaign to bolster and rehabilitate McInnes's reputation while trashing Fraser-Kirk, and some months after his departure from the job he was appointed to another senior role in retailing. Fraser-Kirk was not so fortunate.

But there's more to this widespread blame game that I've found is willingly endorsed by many women. When I began to research this topic I discovered it's quite common for hierarchies, such as many workplaces with well-defined power groups, to foster what is known as 'horizontal violence', which results in paying out on your colleagues. Psychological and sociological theory about dominant and oppressed cohorts bears out the tendency for those in subordinate groups to turn their frustration at their unfair treatment onto each other rather than those in charge. Horizontal violence is used to describe inter-group conflict or hostility, which is associated with oppressed groups, according to research by academic Carolyn Hastie, which looks at the problem in nursing.

'Self-expression and autonomy is controlled by forces with greater prestige, power and status than themselves', she writes. This kind of behaviour is the 'inappropriate way oppressed people release built-up tension when they are unable to address and solve issues with the oppressor'. It is, in fact, part of the dynamics around a sense of powerlessness. Horizontal violence is common in workplace cultures, Hastie points out. It is a form of bullying and acts to socialise those who are different into the status quo, and in the workplace is the result of many factors, including the ideology associated with the socialisation of males and females in western culture.

According to what psychologists call social dominance theory, members are more likely to engage in behaviours that damage their group if the collective is subordinate rather than dominant. This includes violence towards members of the group, according to psychologist Simon Moss. When women are told their own behaviour is causing their problems in male-dominated workplaces, then perhaps they will be more likely to exhibit this behaviour. Even the myth that women need to be attractive has been shown to evoke a perception of themselves as sexual objects that compromises performance, according to Moss. There are also research studies that show women who reach senior roles tend to mirror the norms of this cohort to fit in, as Jayne Hrdlicka described, to avoid too much more attention.

This kind of analysis suggests relying on generalisations that women are just naturally bitchy to each other is inadequate and unfounded, given the complexity of gender and behaviour patterns in hierarchies. I liked the way writer and columnist Caitlin Moran expressed her view on this issue in 2011:

> When people suggest that what, all along, has been holding women back is *other women,* bitching about each other, I think they're severely overestimating the power of a catty zinger during a fag break. We have to remember that snidely saying 'Her hair's a bit limp on top' isn't what's keeping womankind from closing the 30 per cent pay gap and a place on the board of directors. I think that's more likely to be down to tens of thousands of years of ingrained social, political and economic misogyny and the patriarchy [to be honest]. That's just got slightly more leverage than a gag about someone's bad trousers.

The fact is lousy stuff happens at work, regardless of gender. But labelling women the core problem for their female colleagues is an unsubstantiated cul-de-sac that plays off classic stereotypes. I have seen women bitch about each other and men do the same thing. I've seen women in management under enormous pressure to perform and nurture women too, then criticised for playing favourites. I've watched women being told to show more confidence, then get slammed for being too ambitious and difficult. None of this is easy to understand, much less deal with in a busy workplace. But one thing I know: the small numbers of women in management and senior jobs simply don't have the power to suppress an entire generation of skilled women from rising up the ranks in the same way as their male colleagues.

It is a myth that fine-tuning your behaviour in the workplace by wearing clothes and acting tough to resemble a notional male version of success will really change much for women. And blaming other women for the lion's share of gender barriers in the workplace doesn't really add up either. I think there has to be much more discussion about these myths and the bias with which all of us view the world to flush out the dodgy premises they are based on. It seems to me that debunking the alpha male model as a pathway to success would be a good place to start and help shed a stack of unhelpful gender generalisations that hamper men as much as women. The reliance on the deficit model tells us that despite the rhetoric, organisations haven't shifted their notions of what a good worker looks like much at all and being simply female remains a basic inhibitor. This kind of pigeonholing of half the human race is a ridiculously clumsy way of negotiating complex social and business systems and it's getting us nowhere fast.

CASE STUDY: NAB

National Australia Bank's (NAB's) business banking division began running a series of advertisements in 2009 inviting women to seminars on banking as a career. Several women who attended the first seminar were recruited by the bank, which was also able to compile a handy database of potential women recruits, and, of course, wave the flag for NAB at the same time.

The program has rather neatly circumvented some of the barriers that may exist internally for women candidates, and it has transformed the approach to hiring, according to NAB business banking head Joseph Healy.

It allows us to access women who wouldn't normally find their way through into the bank. Then we have a pool of women who know us and it reduces the costs and risks associated with hiring and could make a significant impact on gender diversity. Businesses screen out certain people and we never solve this problem through normal channels.

Half my leadership team are women. And we have had a program of hiring 200 bankers this year (2010). We've set ourselves a goal of 50–50 women and there's no shortage of women.

NAB expects 500 to 600 women to go through the seminars each year throughout Australia, and is finding many attendees are highly educated but under-employed. However, recruiting the women is one thing, supporting them is another. That's more of a challenge, but Healy says progress on gender equity is now woven into the performance management process.

> For general managers and above it's in their diversity score card. You can't get a score of four or above if you have not demonstrated personal leadership on gender diversity. A lot of men said, 'OK, but how do we do this?' I feel that the resistance was almost a cultural one of 'we don't know how to make this work'.
>
> Change agents are working throughout the organisation with senior managers on different approaches. And the business bank has also mandated that recruitment panels have to have at least one woman on the candidate shortlist.

MYTH 7:

TIME WILL HEAL ALL

When I interviewed Martin Parkinson, secretary to the Australian Treasury, about a recent study on women in the department, he explained how his thinking on this subject had changed. Like many senior executives in organisations he had hoped that over time the poor representation of women at senior levels would correct itself. After many years of observing the rising number of female graduates joining the department but little change in executive numbers he started to realise that the idea of the growing pipeline of well-educated women that would automatically transform gender ratios throughout organisations needed to be re-examined. He had thought the lack of gender diversity was a cohort issue, meaning his department only had to wait until there were enough women in the pipeline and they would move up through the system into the senior executive service or SES.

> Increasingly, I think you become convinced
> that a lot of the things we had done – improved

access to part-time work and childcare facilities
– were important but ad hoc responses. There
was something more deeply seated than if we sat
around and waited the market would sort it out.
I could see the cohort getting bigger and bigger in
the '90s with women coming out of economics,
then it was the pipeline and thinking the problem
would solve itself ... In 2011 we've had very high
proportion of females being able to be recruited
into Treasury over time. If it's not fixed itself,
then why not? We have got some issues around
unconscious bias and job design and how we
manage part-time work and these are things we
have to tackle. We don't say we have the answers.
The objective is to deepen the pool of leaders.

Quite a few experienced women leave Treasury when
they are just below the senior executive level, he said.
Sometimes they cite family commitments and uncon-
sciously that was a rationale accepted by senior management for many years, but it's not just that, he now
believes.

I honestly don't know, but I suspect when I
look back I think I've made a series of implicit
judgements at various times in my career about
other people, saying that it makes sense for her
to leave Treasury or the workplace because of

young children. I think it's too convenient an explanation.

Treasury has now set a target of 35 per cent women in the SES by 2016 and he hopes that will help push some more concerted action, including looking at job redesign, so that roles typically seen as full-time only can be restructured. Parkinson notes that the public sector does better than the private sector on representation, but it's not about a certain part of the economy. 'I don't think it's a sectoral problem but a societal problem that manifests itself in different ways. Whether we hit 35 per cent or not, it will mean over the next four to five years there will be some pretty interesting and rewarding outcomes.'

The targets set by Treasury will bring it into line with a number of well-known organisations that have also come to realise the pipeline that promised to deliver a steady flow of women into all parts of organisations and society hasn't delivered. In fact, despite its popularity the pipeline has qualified as a myth for many decades, and continues to be quoted on a regular basis. It seems as though each successive generation believes it has uncovered that the key to progress is just to sit and wait for the natural flow of women to emerge. This rather assumes that the requisite changes to attitude will by default also occur as barriers melt away in front of women. We simply don't have much evidence to suggest this has or ever will happen. It reminds me of Albert Einstein's saying that the definition of insanity is doing the same thing over and over again and expecting different results.

Part of the pipeline's allure is that it sounds obvious, logical and not too confronting. It doesn't bring to mind radical change or pushing people out of comfort zones, but a gentle partial changing of the guard. As such, it can be a handy way to fob off those wanting more overt action and get the naysayers off your back as well. And look at the data: more women are participating in the Australian workforce than ever before. Women make up 45.6 per cent per cent of paid workers according to EOWA data, and the ratio has continued to rise over the last few decades. Women now outnumber men (51 per cent) in the US workforce. Between February 1978 and June 2009 ABS figures show that the Australian labour force participation rate of women increased from 43.5 per cent to 58.7 per cent. so women in jobs now clearly outnumber those who are not employed.

Nevertheless, it is significant that women's presence in paid work remains largely restricted to lower skilled jobs or in white-collar sectors to clerical/mid-management roles. According to a report by Sanders and colleagues for Bain & Company, *What Stops Women from Reaching the Top?*, representation of women in senior executive positions within ASX200 companies has not exceeded 13 per cent for the last decade. A handful of Australian companies, such as MAp Airports, Pacific Brands and Austar United Communications, have achieved gender parity, where it was found that women represent roughly half the executive team. And two of these companies are run by women CEOs – Kerrie Mather at MAp Airports and Sue Morphet at Pacific Brands. There is another 11 per cent that has 'critical mass' – here women represent 25 per cent or more of their senior executive team. However, 62 per cent of ASX200 companies do not have any female senior executives. While disturbing, these statistics are not surprising when you consider that just 15 per cent of the women surveyed by Bain & Company in 2011 believed they had equal opportunity for promotion into senior management positions (down from 20 per cent in 2010), and half of the men surveyed agreed with them.

Despite a lot of hype about our resources-dominated economy having a lot to do with the problem, as Martin Parkinson noted, this poor representation is not confined to a particular sector. But according to academic Marian Baird, professor of employment relations at the University of Sydney, historically there's a pattern in our labour markets that could have some bearing on the current gender representation problems.

We are one of the highest occupationally sex-segregated nations in the world. That may feed into why women go not into the operations areas but into services and support. They are the jobs that get cut in organisations. At the university we see streaming beginning before students enter the workforce. There is a huge majority of females doing an honours degree in HR management and a colleague has 100 per cent men in finance management.

In labour history terms, Baird notes, there may also be some clues in a strong Australian adherence to traditional family structures.

Some of it might arise from a very successful breadwinner model, but this is speculation. It's a model that has broken down, which did mean that men worked and were the breadwinners and had to provide. The women were not expected to earn – there's that heritage in a way. We never got the diversity frameworks the US has. Women tend to work full-time there, and their health benefits are linked to full-time jobs. We do have a very male culture at work – at the shop floor, in meeting rooms and offices. It's very hard to break that.

It is worth noting that the lack of women at the top in Australia is often used to justify their continuing exclusion from such jobs. Instead of examining the barriers to women's advancement, this argument perpetuates the assumption that while women may continue to enter the pipeline they are unable or unwilling to reach levels of experience or tenure necessary for senior roles often attributed to a lack of confidence or ambition (see myth 3). In fact, there is little evidence to support this contention, but there is evidence to show that they progress more slowly than men, even with the same credentials. According to Conseula Pinto and Joan Williams, in 'Hidden gender bias in the workplace',

> Research has shown that men benefit more from their accomplishments than women, and even small imbalances accumulate over time and cause women to advance at a slower rate than men. This phenomenon was tested through a computer simulation of an eight-level institution with equal numbers of men and women employees. The model assumed a 1 per cent bias favoring men. After eight rounds of promotions, the top level of management was composed of 65 per cent men and just 35 per cent women.

The last Australian Census of Women in Leadership,

in 2010, found that women were well represented in middle management ranks in listed companies, but even in sectors where they make up the majority of the workforce there were far fewer women in the senior ranks. The problems are largely systemic, former EOWA executive director Anna McPhee told me when similar statistics were released in 2008. This could no longer be considered an issue of poor supply or the quality of women candidates.

> Women have been graduating in greater numbers than their male peers and working in greater numbers but the executive management group is not reforming. Business has responded and provided that flexibility [that women need], but that moves women from career paths. The impact on a woman's career is disproportionate to the time she is out of the workforce.

So we know women are participating in paid work at increasing levels and they are also making up a growing number of well-educated and experienced professionals. According to the FAHSCIA webpage, 'Improving Women's Economic Wellbeing', in 2009 women made up 64.2 per cent of all higher education graduates. Currently, women account for 55.7 per cent of all higher education students, and 47.6 per cent of all vocational education and training enrolments. In some sectors the ratio is even higher: of those graduating with law degrees, 62 per cent in 2009 were women. These figures are the result of gradual increases in women graduates over the last few decades, but as Baird pointed out, there can be a marked gender difference in areas of study. Courses in engineering and IT, and particularly worryingly, in business schools and MBA degrees, attract far fewer women than men.

When I looked at this a little more closely I was surprised to find just how small the numbers of women MBA students were as the degree is generally regarded as a passport to senior jobs. In fact, most MBA programs not only struggle to enrol women, they also don't include specific gender or women's studies in their curriculum, despite the major gender imbalance still evident at the top of most organisations and the clout of women consumers. A female MBA student told me she was one of 20 women in a cohort of 80 students at a well-known Australian business school, and the only one over 35 years of age. While many of this female cohort have not really encountered overt discrimination in their careers to date, they are yet to face the clashing demands of caring and career due to raising a family, she said.

According to *Financial Review Boss* most Australian business schools have between 20 and 40 per cent women students. Melbourne Business School had

30 per cent women in their full-time course in 2011, Australian School of Business/AGSM 28.8 per cent and University of Technology, Sydney 40.8 per cent. Most of the schools surveyed did not offer a subject devoted to women and management, with a number reporting they covered the topic in one session within a human resources unit. Even if they get to the end of an MBA, international research indicates that women are not gaining the same boost from the degree as male graduates. As I have mentioned, Catalyst found that women MBA graduates in the United States earned an average US$4600 (AU$4300) less than men in their first job after graduation. Men with mentors received US$9260 more in their first post-MBA jobs than women with mentors. For a realm that is supposedly at the cutting edge of organisational research, behaviour and innovation, the lack of women students and courses addressing gender in organisations should be of great concern to business schools and business.

The reasons for the lack of women students give some clues about the pipeline problems too. They include the timing of study, which often overlaps with child-bearing years, the high cost of the courses and the association of an MBA with careers in the male-dominated finance and investment banking sector, according to Penny de Valk, chief executive of the UK's Institute of Leadership and Management. MBA programs adhere to the same 'male breadwinner' model of most businesses, de Valk wrote in a 2011 FT.com article. Because of the obstacles, many women rule themselves out of an MBA and thus out of contention for jobs that require the degree. UK commentator Avivah Wittenberg-Cox wrote in her blog that if business schools were there to satisfy the demands of business, and businesses were genuinely concerned about the gender issue, then presumably that would be reflected in what is researched and taught. 'Arguably business schools have done what business itself has done, namely declared themselves meritocracies and let women come if they so choose.'

Although many UK schools have introduced leadership programs for women, they do not seem to have considered that the issue requires education of the majority of the students – who are men. Wittenberg-Cox points out that because business schools give so little attention to gender in the workplace it becomes even more of a challenge for business to acknowledge and change the causes of the problem. Without the legitimacy of academic attention and research it is also more difficult for those working inside organisations to lobby for change. Business schools need to be more flexible in admissions and improve their marketing to women, said de Valk. Otherwise, the same Catch 22 that hampers women's entry into senior jobs – few female role models and challenges to male norms – will fail to increase women students. The pipeline is suddenly looking even more blocked when you take the business school trend into account.

When I took a look at what was happening with gender representation in the financial services sector in 2010 I found an excellent example of why the pipeline solution is indeed a myth. Australia's finance and insurance industry employed approximately 375 000 employees Australia-wide, according to the EOWA 2006 Industry Vertical study of the sector. The 145 finance and insurance companies reporting annually to EOWA employ over 219 000 employees, of which 59 per cent were female. Women make up 31 per cent of management, placing the industry fifth among other large private-sector industries after the traditional female sectors of education, retail, hospitality and health and community services, but ahead of manufacturing, property and business services. However, the majority of women in the financial services sector are employed in middle- to lower-level occupations, making finance and insurance the third-largest employer of advanced clerical workers and the fifth-largest employer of associate professionals in the total female labour force. There were only two women CEOs and the number of women managers, at 31 per cent, is lower than the average for all sectors of 32 per cent. Given these high levels of women's participation, and the growing number of graduates in related degrees, the proportion of women in finance and insurance management could be considered relatively low when compared with the total proportion of women in the workforce.

It doesn't make sense to argue that there are substantial barriers to entry for women in this white-collar sector. The typical working conditions in financial services organisations are not exactly those of an open-cut mine in remote Australia or a steel mill, or for that matter a factory where some jobs may require levels of physical strength. I have already mentioned the research by DDI Consulting and Catalyst (see myth 1) showing women's progress to be slowed very early on in their careers, and that they have much less chance than men of being identified as potential managers/executives. As a result, they are not offered the same development opportunities as their male colleagues from graduate-entry level. This failure to be included in training, mentoring or secondments acts as a major impediment to entering the pool of candidates for promotion.

Because promotion and recruitment processes are often still opaque in many cases, organisations are not held accountable for gender balance in these areas, according to Ann Howard from DDI. Even having women represented in significant numbers at every leadership level doesn't mean it will carry to the executive level. In fact, there is a backlash against women at the top when they are dominant in leadership roles at every other level, the research found. This back-lash is bolstered by the assumption that as a 'special' group, women should only make up a certain number of the top teams, so if women are already making up a reasonable proportion of junior management they should be satisfied with that and not be greedy. This same mentality is often encountered when conference organisers or media programs are looking for speak-ers and want one or two women involved to ensure their diversity credentials are on show. Suggest a few women for a panel discussion – or even more women than men – and there is shocked resistance.

Women lag behind men in both job level and salary, starting from their first position post-business school, and do not catch up, according to the Cata-lyst report, *The Pipeline's Broken Promise*. When it comes to trusting the pipeline to deliver change at the top it found that 'the assertion that women advance in compensation and level at the same pace as men is overstated and, in many cases, completely wrong'.

Both studies confirm the existence of barriers to women's progress, right from the beginning of their careers, and shed more light on why women are so poorly represented in senior roles, given the growing number of them graduating and entering the work-force. When blockages prevent most qualified women from pursuing the paths into management the solution does not lie in the supply of female employees, but in addressing and dismantling these barriers. Ironically, the scarcity of women in senior ranks leads to further discriminatory attitudes. When a woman does decide to leave a senior job, for example, it often attracts disproportionate attention and leads to an unfortunate belief that her actions are emblematic of her gender's lack of tenacity. This is the 'we tried a woman once and it didn't work' syndrome, which is surprisingly alive and kicking in some business circles.

Those who cling to the hope that time and some new measures will heal all must also be reminded that the only change in this area in the past ten years has been the declining number of women in senior management roles and, until recently, on boards. Even organisations that made some headway in this area in the past, such as Westpac, discovered that small steps in the right direction were easily undone when senior management did not prioritise the issue. The traditional resistance to targets and quotas for women on boards (see myth 5) often hinges on the outdated notion that there are not enough women for the top roles, so poor-quality candidates will be promoted on the basis of gender alone. But the lack of supply argument does not stack up here either. The Women on Boards group says it has about 1500 women out of nearly 8000 members who are board-ready. The mentoring schemes for women aspiring to directorships in 2010–11, including those set up by the AICD and the

Business Council were both over-subscribed.

And how many women are needed? If 40 per cent quotas were to be introduced, the reality is that many boards would be looking for just one or two women. Not really a tall order. Within organisations, targets for women in senior management have not met with the same concerns about lack of supply; perhaps because in many businesses it's hard to ignore the number of women clustering in the middle ranks.

One of the supposed solutions to the blockages in the pipeline is mentoring of promising women by senior executives (usually men). I've already mentioned the popularity of mentoring as a way to boost the number of women on boards and therefore avoid the dreaded spectre of legislated quotas (myth 5). I think the hope is that without rocking the boat too much, mentoring will help nudge the number of women in management higher and crack that wretched glass ceiling. It's a hope that is not well founded. Mentoring programs have been seen as a panacea for women, Karen Morley, co-founder of consulting firm Gender Worx, told me in 2011. 'It's often the first solution to say, "Let's have a mentoring program". The evidence is that many of them don't work.'

Morley's comprehensive review of international and Australian research, *Unlocking the Potential of Women at Work: A Decade of Evidence* in 2010, found plenty of information on the most effective paths for change. Schemes that provide a mentor as a sounding board hold back women's careers, whereas traditional mentoring, which focuses on career paths and finding opportunities, works best. In these pairings the mentor acts as an advocate and progress is tangible. Although the research doesn't establish exactly why current mentoring schemes are ineffective for women, Morley can hazard a guess:

> The kind of support [that is about] easing your troubles soothes and comforts you about what is going on. What that possibly does is collude in keeping women where they are, as opposed to [making you take] a strongly focused look at your next move. That produces results for women. And female mentors have the biggest impact, although the common wisdom is that women need a male mentor.

Morley doesn't recommend that women always choose a female mentor, but she does advocate thinking strategically about a mentor and looking around carefully. In fact, women don't always want to mentor other women. There's a host of reasons for this. I asked Melbourne Business School's Isabel Metz about this perception and she said there is no evidence that women are less likely to help others than their male peers. But she did point out the sheer logistics in business representation means there are just fewer of them and they have a lot of extra pressure and scrutiny to cope with in senior roles. But it can also feed the cliché that women are their own worst enemies, which makes me see red whenever I hear it (see myth 6). I think the sheer frustration of watching decades of female participation in the workforce and a failure to crack the glass ceiling has led to a damaging blame game. Women are told so often that they are the main problem (there's that deficit model again) that they have come to believe it, despite the illogical nature of this thinking. And when they are treated poorly by other women, from whom they expect more support, they become particularly outraged. However, other women are not the main problem, as we have seen from examining the myths – it's established male norms and biased practices that stymie women throughout their careers.

Let's face it, even with the number of potential women leaders in the pipeline there are obviously barely any female role models to look up to, and the few hardy souls who make it continue to attract so much vitriol that their experience is probably more of an inhibitor than a help. This also sets up a Catch 22, as I noted in the column during the damaging Labor leadership stoush in early 2012. Although she won the ballot, the lingering sense of disappointment about Gillard's leadership is not only about her actual performance, but because those expectations of our first woman prime minister have somehow been unfulfilled. This feeds the idea that having a woman in charge has been a failed experiment, not to be repeated in a hurry, which is about as sensible as saying redheads shouldn't apply in future either.

People don't vote for someone just because of their gender, although it may be one factor that is taken into account. But the symbolism of being 'the first' has been hard to ignore. One of the flurry of polls released found that 94 per cent of about 500 women surveyed by the Heat Group agreed that Gillard should not be treated differently as prime minister, but 60 per cent felt she was treated differently to former leaders. Just 9 per cent, however, were very satisfied with how she 'supports the needs of women'. Although it's not clear what this means, it does show the particular pressure Gillard confronts as the first woman prime minister, and the burden of carrying so many expectations. In the business sector the handful of women who run large companies or sit on boards are often subjected to intense scrutiny and judgement. Sue Morphet, CEO of Pacific Brands, copped some very personal criticism of her leadership when the company moved some of its production facilities offshore, leaving many employees without a job. Although this kind of restructuring is not rare in Australia, and male CEOs are also targets for criticism, the level of the response was disproportionate to most other examples. Similarly, a few years ago NAB director Catherine Walter resigned from the prestigious role after the fallout from a foreign exchange trading scandal at the bank. The ructions on the board involved Walter's reputation being called into question, and she was described as a highly ambitious 'career woman' who asked too many questions at meetings and didn't agree with her colleagues. What an unforgiveable combination! This kind of damaging coverage is another reason women find the climb to the top so fraught, and the pipeline theory doesn't stack up. The struggles of women in power to negotiate age-old ideas about leadership mean there's no inevitable flow of females into those top echelons.

However, the hard work and pressure that delivered progress on board representation in Australia shows that when there is a will to change women will be found. There are many outstanding women in corporate Australia – Jillian Broadbent, former investment banker; director, Carolyn Hewson, who sits on several boards and is regarded as one of the country's most influential directors; Jillian Segal, ASX director; Nicole Hollows, CEO of Macarthur Coal; Ann Sherry, CEO of Carnival Australia; and others mentioned throughout this book. And there are many more working across senior ranks and in sectors such as professional services, health, and academia. They are role models within and beyond their organisations and have proved to be generous supporters of other women.

Most of these women would like to see a better gender mix, not least because the novelty of being a woman in power would dissipate. Normalising women's presence at the table takes off the pressure, and makes the notion that the performance of one woman somehow reflects the capacity of her entire gender start to seem pretty silly. This is why reaching a critical mass of about 33 per cent women has been shown to dissolve many gender biases while ensuring they are no longer regarded as a minority group. We need to highlight these examples and successful teams because Gillard's tenure has shown that it is a hardy woman indeed who steps up to be the first of her gender in a high-profile role. Despite the number of women ministers in the federal government it's sobering to realise there are fewer women in federal parliament in 2012 than there were before the 2010 federal election, with a drop from 27.3 per cent to 24.7 per cent. In this case there may well be a genuine pipeline problem for the future, although it's hard to blame women for being put off by the prospect of a political career.

When it comes to women on boards, the pipeline myth still manages to effectively prop up the arguments against quotas, examined in myth 5, although this can also get a bit confusing. On the one hand, those against quotas say the problems are to do with the lack of qualified women – a supply problem – and therefore a higher risk of tokenism. On the other hand, they also tend to argue that there's no need for quotas as voluntary measures and the pipeline will result in more women naturally being appointed directors. But the latter conclusion does imply the women are available and just haven't been identified or supported as potential board members. This is exactly why advocates see no alternative to legislative change, because so little has been achieved in recent decades and a wide gap remains between rhetoric and reality. It's worth noting that in 2009 only 5 per cent of board appointments were women, while in 2011 women made up 29 per cent of new board directors. It seems that in a relatively short period of time plenty of qualified women were discovered – it just took some active searching and a different approach to development and recruitment to actually recognise them. No pipeline was ever going to transform boards in that timeframe.

Lastly, there's another version of the pipeline myth that has to do with generational change. Stop worrying about the problems with lack of women at the top or the gender pay gap, I've been told by many a CEO, because the next group of corporate executives are from a different generation and they will ensure that change occurs. It should be said, some of these very well-known people are convinced that this is the case. They believe they have a very different attitude to the stuffy traditionalists who went before them and therefore their peers are all enlightened too, and will follow through on some difficult and deeply unpopular changes to improve women's lot when they are the main group in charge.

It's the same at the forums I speak to on a regular basis. Some young man or woman will invariably comment that they and their cohort are different and they get it. They claim they are gender blind, so why would it be any different in the workplace? They know what has to happen to ensure better gender balance and sharing of the domestic load and they will do it. They really mean it – I know that. But I'm afraid I'm not convinced. Perhaps it's my age and hanging around this space a few decades, but something tells me that relying on a new group of managers to tackle some very tough issues or enlightenment to win out over ambition, pride and avarice, is not a sound risk avoidance strategy. In fact, it sounds like an excuse to do pretty much nothing at all, and we just don't have any evidence to suggest that a lack of action or agitation has helped the justice of the gender equity argument to resonate in organisations. Quite the opposite, I'd say. The fact that I've heard this rationale for 35 years and seen quite limited results for the better – but I have seen the odd back-sliding – bolsters my proposition.

My scepticism about the imminent changing of the guard leading to greater gender equity was reinforced when I watched the film about the founding of Facebook, *The Social Network*, and read a profile of Sheryl Sandberg, the chief operating officer of the company. The film is, of course, a piece of fiction to some extent, but it does depict a very male environment where even the original reason for setting up Facebook was explained as a way to compare the hottest young women on campus at Harvard. All the main protagonists, who go on to make a fortune in the social media, are men. This is a sector synonymous with youth and a new generation, but women, once again, seem to be largely peripheral. Out in the real world, the IT sector looks remarkably similar to its movie depiction. Certainly in the upper echelons, it is heavily male dominated according to Ken Auletta's profile of Sandberg, 'A women's place'.

> Among the hottest new companies – Facebook, Twitter, Zynga, Groupon, Foursquare – none, as Kara Swisher reported in the blog, 'All things digital', has a female director on its board. PayPal has no women on its five-member board; Apple has one of seven; Amazon one of eight; Google two of nine. When I asked Mark Zuckerberg why

his five-member board has no women, his voice, which is normally loud, lowered to a whisper: 'We have a very small board.' He went on, 'I'm going to find people who are helpful, and I don't particularly care what gender they are or what company they are. I'm not filling the board with check boxes.' (He recently added a sixth member: another man.) The venture-capital firms that support new companies have even sharper imbalances; Sequoia Partners lists eighteen partners on its Web site, none of them women.

One reason there are so few female executives in Silicon Valley is that few women become engineers, with women making up less than 20 per cent of engineering and computer-science majors in the United States. 'For girls, there is a stigma attached to engineering, Marissa Mayer, who is now a vice-president at Google, says. 'They don't want to become the stereotype of all-night coders, hackers with pasty skin.' Michelle Hutton, president of the international Computer Science Teachers Association, says, 'Computer science is seen as a very masculine thing' – just 'as girls don't want to be garbage collectors because that's seen as a boys' thing.' In Australia only about a third of total IT employees are women and the number in senior executive roles is very small.

So Sandberg stands out as an exception, and while

she doesn't consider herself a feminist, she has set up a women's network and speaks publicly about the need for more women to enter the sector. She advised women in a speech to the TEDwomen conference in 2010 to be more proactive, negotiate more and go for senior jobs before having breaks for kids (see 'Myth-busting and beyond'). But her comments also attracted criticism for making some assumptions based on several myths, including the meritocracy and pipeline beliefs.

Marie Wilson, the founder of the White House Project, which promotes women for leadership positions, attended Sandberg's TED speech and knows and admires her. But, Wilson says, 'underneath Sheryl's assessment is the belief that this is a meritocracy. It's not.' Courage and confidence alone will not compensate when male leaders don't give women opportunities. She adds, 'Women are not dropping out to have a child. They're dropping out because they have no opportunity.'

And she doesn't agree that new attitudes can close the gender gap. Sylvia Ann Hewlett, who directs the Gender and Policy program at Columbia, read Sandberg's speech and took exception. Hewlett agrees with Sandberg that women must be more assertive, but she believes Sandberg simply doesn't understand that there is a 'last glass ceiling,' created not by male sexists but by 'the lack of sponsorship,' senior executives who persistently advocate for someone to move up.

There is nevertheless a wonderful story in Sandberg's success and her efforts to support other women. But some of the barriers she has surmounted would not be easily challenged by less capable – or, in her case, outstanding – women. And the outlook for women in IT and the applied sciences is not great in Australia. Women make up one in three IT students, and at the other end of the scale, just 50 of the 800 fellows of the Australian Academy of Technological Sciences and Engineering are women.

It is also apparent that not all hope of generational change is unfounded. I was struck by the comment of a man attending a forum run by CEDA on women's leadership:

Another issue males need to understand is that baby boomers are still in charge and they don't understand women as much as they think they do. An example of this is a baby boomer CEO of a top 10 company a few years ago who was about to hire a woman into a position one below him. The woman confided in the recruiter that she was pregnant and the recruiter informed somebody in the organisations who ultimately informed the CEO. The whole process nearly collapsed, except a 39-year-old man at the time said, 'This is ridiculous, that's fine, I'll hire her'. The interesting

> part is the 58-year-old CEO had absolutely no
> intention of hiring her; this was a deal breaker.
> I think baby boomers are really struggling with
> issues that the next generation are not struggling
> with as much.

Hopefully that is the case and men with different views are encouraged to challenge such traditional thinking. I'm not a complete doom and gloom merchant about human nature by the way, but there's something about formal hierarchies where livings are earned, pay and power are negotiated, along with status and even identity these days, that keeps propping up the old attitudes. Fiddling around with who gets the next step ahead, the pay rise, the rewards and promotions along the way, is volatile stuff and can bring out the worst in people. I have often wondered if some of my colleagues' families would recognise and approve of their loved ones' behaviour at the office. There can be something quite Darwinian about the modern workplace and when gender comes into the mix it gets really messy, confronting us all with deep-seated biases and beliefs about the order of things. Those who have benefited from the system usually see little reason to radically change the way things work, and that includes men and women.

Changing all this is difficult and scary. But resistance is not due to businesses being laggards that sit apart from social change, but the fact that organisations are a core part of society and therefore help to form and reflect the standards and mores in our culture. You can't change the workplace for women unless society starts to really shift the onus away from women as the standard bearers of domesticity and child care. Reduce the housework load that faces women and the demands of the workplace would be a very different proposition for them. Change the workplace demands on men and the home-front would be a different place for women.

So the idea that a wave of generational change will automatically transform business places into fairer environments is probably lazy or wishful thinking. Just as dodgy is the notion that change for the better will continue in the way it has at times over the last century. Social change never smoothly transitions through a series of predictable stages and feminism has been a great case study of this observation. The pioneering suffragettes, such as the Pankhursts, would probably find today's social standards for women astounding in many ways and disappointing in others. Internationally, women's emancipation has advanced in some parts of the world and remains a pipedream in others, where women are not even allowed to attend school or drive a car.

I remember interviewing US feminist and consultant to Goldman Sachs, Laura Liswood, and she said it was dangerous to assume progress would continue in any arena. In some ways we have been lulled by the great technological changes over the last 20 years to assume that new development will continue and be positive, she pointed out (and how ironic to find that the very sector that is producing such change has shifted so little in its gender composition). This is just not what history tells us. And feminism is a movement that shows sometimes one step forward is accompanied by two backwards.

The pipeline has patently not delivered the transformation it promised and yet it is offered up as a serious solution by business executives all the time. In dismantling it we should also reiterate that the goal to get more women in senior roles does indeed make a difference to representation in other ranks, no matter what the conjecture or assumptions. Key findings from a major longitudinal study released in early 2012 show that an increase in the share of female top managers is associated with subsequent increases in the share of women in mid-level management positions within firms, and this result is robust to controlling for firm size, workforce composition, federal contractor status, firm fixed effects, year fixed effects, and industry-specific trends, as described by Fridan A Kurtulus and Donald Tomaskovic-Devey.

Improved recognition and nurturing of professional women from the beginning of their careers, and encouragement to articulate their goals would alleviate some of the barriers. Researchers for Catalyst asked CEOs and executives from major companies for suggestions on what to do to shift the gender impasse, and their study's findings included: don't assume that the playing field has been levelled; re-design systems to correct early inequities; collect and review salary growth metrics; build in checks and balances against unconscious bias; make assignments based on qualifications, not presumptions.

Just don't think it will all unfold naturally and in a few years. I would hardly be an advocate for gender equity if I were a complete pessimist, but it is important to keep up the activism or watch a default to the old, comfortable and grossly inequitable ways. The gender picture may well have changed, but possibly for the worst and we know that can occur because it happened in Australia between 2006 and 2008. The pipeline has been revealed as a fraudulent excuse.

CASE STUDY: McDONALD'S

In late 2009 I profiled the senior women in the executive team at McDonald's and described some of the reasons for the company's success in balancing the gender mix at the top. While some of the women are no longer in these roles, the mix remains close to 46 per cent women in 2012 and the analysis makes a good case for getting senior men to advocate for change.

McDonald's Australia's strong results in recent times and even during the financial crisis have been the work of a management team that is two-thirds female. Catriona Noble, managing director of McDonald's Australia, knows why there is a sizeable group of women around the table when the leadership team of the fast-food giant meets. Consecutive CEOs – all men – made this a top priority.

Their legacy, inherited and bolstered by current CEO Peter Bush, means that McDonald's is one of the rare businesses in Australia where 67 per cent of the top team are women. By comparison, women hold just 8 per cent of key management roles in all S&P/ASX200 companies. This is not just unusual for Australia, but stands out in the Macdonald's worldwide network. Noble notes:

> I was just at a [global] women's leadership conference for McDonald's and there were 300 women and 45 were from Australia. It was a mixture of our corporate team and some of our female owner-operators and partners. I did a talk about using Australia as a case study.

Far from being seen by their international peers as an anomaly, Noble says, the Australian women were sharing their experience with male counterparts, who were keen to see how it was done.

At the announcement of Noble's appointment to managing director in 2008, CEO Peter Bush said she was the first female managing director of one of the US-based company's 'big 10', or largest subsidiaries in revenue and earnings. Noble says:

> We [women] make up 67 per cent of the senior team. If you look at the general [workforce], it is 46 per cent. It's a great retention strategy. When women lead, everybody sees that people are advancing on merit and at every level. It's empowering.
>
> It's a high-performance work environment. People aren't hung up on how we do that. There's no regard for presenteeism. Here it is calibrated that if you can do your job in a flexible way, then do it. They're still working hard, but in a way that works for them.

It's still most unusual to hear success attributed to having a diverse top team – rather than despite one. And no magic wand was involved.

> It came about through men primarily – it's necessary to make the change from the top. Peter Ritchie, the founding CEO in Australia in the 1970s and '80s, had a focus on people and training and set the people strategies. Then Charlie Bell took on diversity and

looked at ways to change how roles were performed, and he was a great people person. But I think the real change came with Guy Russo [in the late 1990s]; he was the real champion of women's leadership and embraced progressive work practices. And he led by example. Sometimes you can talk the talk, but people will do as you do, not as you say.

Russo, in particular, went out of his way to attend his children's school sports days and do tuckshop duty, showing that flexibility was not about gender, but a different way of working. Noble recalls:

Everyone knew he was focused on results, but he showed it was about achieving business outcomes in flexible ways. He made it much easier for women to be effective. Bushy says we are gender blind ... It's the work of the previous people that means he can say that. It's easy not to focus on gender.

In fact, it's well documented that once a critical mass – about 40 per cent – is reached in a group, the difference (whether it is race, gender or creed) recedes as a focus. Most of the women on the senior team agree that they don't think much about gender at work. But they also understand that their presence at the top sends a clear message to younger women – and men – about progression and a different way of doing things. That includes juggling home and work, as several of the women have young children.

> What I love about this team is the real variety. Some are married with children and some single. I'm pleased there's a bunch of different role models. The reality for a lot of women – it is not a corporate issue – is that women who have children still tend to carry the load, and until we get men who want to play that role it's very difficult.

McDonald's Australia has pioneered successful developments, such as healthy options in menus and listing ingredients on packaging. None of the women executives would suggest the strategy was down to them, or are the direct result of 'female' thinking. But they represent an important part of the consumer base, Noble says, and mothers are key decision-makers about family diets and outings.

There is also a strong sense of loyalty among the McDonald's senior team, several of whom started with the chain more than 20 years ago. It's been more than 25 years since Noble started as a part-time crew member. Operations director Raylee McLeod has been with the company the same number of years. Other colleagues – supply chain director Jackie McArthur, regional manager Joanne Taylor, marketing director Helen Farquhar and public affairs director Kristene Mullen – joined more recently, but have already chalked up tenure that is unusual in any organisation these days.

This may well be the result of the company's career options. Although an operations background has helped forge a number of senior managers' careers, Noble points out that it's not a path closed to those with specialist skills. She has made it a priority to move some women in her team into line roles to broaden their experience.

> Joanne [Taylor] is an HR specialist who came in five years ago. That's not something in the past we would have done in McDonald's: bring people in for a senior role and then put them into an operational level. She went into a director of franchise role and regional manager.

Farquhar, with a marketing background forged at Procter & Gamble, is also being groomed for wider responsibilities. 'She came in as national marketing manager and is also doing her operational training with a view to move into a bigger and better role,' Noble says. 'She's a marketing expert – they love the accountability of line management. That's where it's at. It's a P&L and they get excited.'

Another unusual career path is that of McArthur, who studied aeronautical engineering and is now director of supply chain, managing about 40 people and a $900 million budget. She also has responsibility for product development.

There are barriers to this kind of change, Noble says, such as establishing different work patterns and accommodation of flexibility. But the rewards are tangible:

> We've found we have been able to grow the business
> – not just through having women but having a
> better blend ... but it's got to mean more than just
> thinking it's a good thing to do. It does take a lot of
> compromise and flexibility on what you will tolerate.

MYTH-BUSTING
AND BEYOND

Four women from three states are running an
online campaign that has already swayed several
big brands to pull thousands of dollars' worth
of advertising from Southern Cross Austereo's
'Kyle and Jackie O Show'. The 'Sack Vile
Kyle' campaign began in late November when,
originally, five women who did not know each
other got together online and decided to pressure
as many brands as possible to stop advertising on
Sandilands's radio show. In less than two months,
Sack Vile Kyle has lobbied through Facebook,
Twitter, blogs and emails to sway eight brands
to pull advertising from the show: Jenny Craig,
Mazda Australia, Kia Australia, OPSM, Aussie
Home Loans, Warner Bros. Movie World, Sony
Australia and Spotlight. 'It's a cause we all believe
in,' said Heather Carr, 30, from Townsville, who
founded the group with four women – who she
still hasn't met – living in different states.

'"Sack Vile Kyle" campaign drives sponsors away',
Jonathan Swan, *Sydney Morning Herald*, 20 January 2012

This report followed radio host Kyle Sandilands's on-air attack in late 2011 on a female journalist who had criticised his recently aired television special. For her efforts she was called 'a fat slag' and told to watch her mouth or Sandilands would hunt her down. It wasn't the first time the radio personality had courted controversy, and many of his outbursts have been directed at women, but this was the straw that broke the camel's back. The repercussions included condemnation and protests from across society. The successful 'Sack Vile Kyle' campaign was particularly carefully aimed to add some extra potency by lobbying the advertisers who sponsored Sandilands's radio show. These are large companies with substantial advertising budgets that few media companies can afford to lose, even if they are blasé about offending their women listeners. A couple of months after the Kyle debacle, a similar scenario in the United States saw conservative radio host Rush Limbaugh lose a number of his well-known sponsors after he called a woman student, who was campaigning to have contraception included on employer health insurance schemes, a slut and a prostitute.

These days there is increasing awareness in the business world of the risk from a product boycott or trashed reputation when poor practices are alleged, such as accusations that Nike used contractors employing child labour in the developing world to manufacture expensive sports shoes; or association with overt sexism. The 'Sack Vile Kyle' women knew very well they had leverage through women's collective buying power to trigger a consumer backlash. It seems to me they were also doing some handy myth-busting of the idea that women believe they are living in a post-feminist world where opportunities are open to all and sexism is a thing of the past. They are representative of a new activism that probably wouldn't label itself feminist, although that's exactly what it is: they are the social media era's suffragettes whose fight may not be for the vote, but is nonetheless a crusade against misogyny. By hitting the hip pocket nerve they put a neat modern twist on the continuing struggles for women to be treated fairly and with respect. Call it what you will, but that's a fight with a lot of heritage.

These days women have so much more ability to coordinate and mount these kinds of campaigns, through access to social media, which is just as well. The gist of Sandilands's comments, attacking his critic and not her criticism, could have come from another era altogether, when women were almost absent from most public forums and it was only the odd brave woman who spoke out, often attracting ridicule. However, Sandilands's continuing popularity is a reminder of how some some parts of Australian culture remain decidedly male-oriented with a strong adherence to old-fashioned gender stereotypes. This comes as quite a shock to many people who move here from overseas, and our business culture is also seen by many to be outdated and alarmingly sexist. A highly skilled woman who arrived here from the United States a few years ago described how astonished she was to encounter such overt discrimination in the job market. She was told by a leading headhunter that she would never get a similar salary in the Australian market because she was female. (He was wrong – she did.)

Luckily, it's not just women who are affronted by this kind of casual sexism that is still manifest in our supposedly egalitarian society. When I spoke about the reaction and outcry about Sandilands at a management forum held by Microsoft in Sydney in late 2011, to my surprise most of the audience – roughly 70 per cent men – applauded. I didn't assume men would be condoning the comments, but I was surprised by the strength of their objections. That's a cause for optimism.

Mobilising the people who evidently find the oafish Sandilands offensive is not the same as tackling the overt and covert barriers for women in the workplace, although it does serve as a potent lesson in one important way. Focusing on how the myths hamper women can help remind business of the enormous advantages from recognising the clout women have as consumers and employees. When 'Sack Vile Kyle' lobbied the advertisers their message was a warning shot designed to remind them of this power and why it should not be taken for granted. It's a sad addendum that the company employing Sandilands, Southern Cross, stated that the incident had 'a minor effect' on profits. There may be other less tangible costs arising from the event.

Unpicking the myths shows there is many a workplace that could benefit from a reminder of the message 'Sack Vile Kyle' sent to the advertisers, instead of wasting the talents of half the population. The trick is how to deliver it. In reality none of us can afford to spit the dummy or upset the applecart too much when we are in paid work, for fear of penalties or even losing our jobs. That's why a gradual but consistent dismantling of the common misconceptions, while not as dramatic as the 'Sack Vile Kyle' efforts, is an important and practical adjunct to other formal efforts to challenge the political, social and organisational gender norms. It's worth reminding ourselves of the Margaret Mead idea: 'a small group of thoughtful people could change the world. Indeed it's the only thing that ever has.'

That small group is not confined to women, as the Microsoft experience showed. Earlier in the book I mentioned my exasperation with the recent corporate obsession with unconscious bias, and the need to approach some of this activity with a degree of scepticism. My views were actually echoed by a senior executive at ANZ, who also saw the drawbacks of this particular approach. There's a risk that focusing on unconscious bias avoids the very real and more pressing problem of conscious bias, according to ANZ Banking Group executive Nigel Williams, at a forum on gender I attended in 2011. Williams is a senior executive at ANZ, has been on the bank's diversity council for seven years and jointly leads its Gender Action Network, aimed at getting women into leadership positions.

There's plenty of work still to be done to get ANZ to where it should be, he told me after the forum, but focusing on unconscious bias is not the way to go.

> My view is, I do agree there's unconscious bias, but it's like saying 'I'm not a racist, but ...' As a result, you get into excuses and it's a euphemism. Everyone is frustrated they haven't made a difference [to gender representation] and is looking for the silver bullet, and it feels like unconscious bias is the bullet, but I don't think it is.

By making these generalisations about bias you are giving people excuses instead of addressing the problem, and some better scrutiny should be applied to overt practices that act as deterrents to women, he said. If every off-site meeting you have is at a golf course where men and women spend the afternoon playing off a different tee, you need to watch your team-building. If all your team meetings start with talk about AFL then you are excluding people. Or a decision to go abseiling for team bonding is a conscious decision you make and we excuse it by saying we are unconscious and we haven't thought about it, he pointed out. 'If a senior manager sat down and was saying "I hadn't thought about competition law or regulation or accounting policy", what would we say?' In attempting to change thinking in business, sometimes the myths are actually being propped up rather than dismantled by these efforts, as Williams explained. He could see the problem and the bias against women quite clearly and consciously.

He's not the only one, and there are some other glimmers of light and good examples from a range of organisations highlighted in the case studies throughout this book, although none would make great claims about their efforts so far. It's been a habit of mine to try and highlight as many success stories in the business world as possible in 'Corporate Woman' because it has been very clear from feedback that the best way to move ahead is by learning from others. An example from a well-known company legitimises these efforts and luckily the pool of examples is growing and often comes from unexpected sectors, such as resources. They remind us of how formal levers, along with some myth-busting and behavioural change, can work together to deliver results.

A few years ago these examples simply weren't around, and the formation of a group of heavy-hitting CEOs to form a Male CEO Champions of Change group would have been seen as a ridiculous overreaction. As the myths make clear, until quite recently the common response to most queries about the gender issue was 'what problem?' Started up in 2010 by Sex Discrimination Commissioner Elizabeth Broderick, the symbolism of the group is powerful, and shows some formal commitment to the agenda from the top end of town. However, they have quite a lot of ground to cover after much neglect. When the 11 chief executives and company chairpersons sat side by side on stage at the Male CEO Champions of Change lunch in Sydney in late 2011 they were talking about why they have made gender equity a priority, and pledged to be public advocates. But a few blocks away Business Council of Australia (BCA) president Graham Bradley was giving a speech titled 'Productivity or complacency: Which path for Australia's future?' He aired concerns that Australia was on the path of complacency and noted the BCA was encouraging government to boost workforce participation for older Australians, Indigenous Australians, and other 'under-represented' groups.

There was no mention of the productivity boost

for the economy if business finally tackled Australia's entrenched gender imbalance. And even though the CEOs have made a historically important commitment and argue the same business case rationale for change, they acknowledge only minor progress. The truth is, we fail every day at not creating more inclusive cultures, said Telstra CEO David Thodey, and it's time for honest conversations on the issues. But intentions are one thing, action is another. As the champions appreciate, this is a business problem that is highly resistant to change. The tendency is to quarantine gender as some sort of special agenda but women's participation is fundamental to all conversations about economic growth and productivity.

This is why entrenched business practices that maintain the myths remain such a serious inhibitor, and not just for women. The deeper issue is a massive corporate mis-adaptation to today's talent realities and the subsequent inability to retain and develop women as well as men, according to Avivah Wittenberg-Cox on her blog in 2010.

> I call this 'gender asbestos'. It's hidden in
> the walls, cultures and mindsets of many
> organizations. But ridding the structure of the
> toxins will require more than pointing accusingly
> at the mess. It requires a detailed plan for how

to move forward – and a compelling, attractive portrait of the result.

Many executives in businesses around the world are uninformed about the shifts taking place in labour force participation, such as the decline of prime-age US men in work to just over 80 per cent from 95 per cent in the 1960s. They either don't know or ignore the fact that women are estimated to represent a growth market twice as big as India and China combined, she pointed out. Her suggestion is to focus on solutions and stop asking, 'What's wrong with women that they're not making it to the top?' Start asking, "What's wrong with companies if they can't retain and promote the majority of educated Americans, and can't adequately satisfy the majority of US consumers?" Only the right questions can yield effective answers.' In Australia, the right questions have yet to be asked consistently at the top, despite some moves to mainstream the gender equity discussion. The young men and women who will make up executive ranks in the future must also start asking these questions and be part of this process, as the pipeline myth reminds us.

At one of the male champions meetings they watched a presentation by a group of boys from Sydney Boys High who, as part of their Community Action Project in 2010, chose to create an awareness-raising project for UN Women Australia, targeting gender inequality (the project was managed by High Resolves, a not-for-profit group that runs educational programs for high school students). They were particularly shocked to hear that women own 2 per cent of property worldwide, that 40 million female babies and girls have gone missing in China, and that one in three women is beaten or sexually abused in her lifetime. They were also surprised to learn that only 24 per cent of parliamentary seats are held by women in the Australian House of Representatives.

Watching the short video they made about the project it's clear most of the boys originally thought there was no problem or that it had been solved long ago. Lee Martin, High Resolves program manager for Sydney Boys High, said the boys' first reaction was 'why should we care?' Then two things really changed their minds. One was the statistics on women's work, wages, representation and as victims of violence. The second was the 'girl effect', which shows that supporting girls and women improves society for all. The video of the project has had more than 3000 hits on YouTube and has been viewed around the world, according to Roya Baghai, co-founder of High Resolves. These young men's conversion proves myth-busting is both needed and that it works.

I had a similar experience when I spoke to a group of employees at an investment bank about the evidence rebutting the myths and the status of women in the business sector. A young man in the audience was the first to ask a question and wanted to know why universities were not teaching this topic and raising awareness? He was obviously surprised and dismayed by the data. No matter how many times I present this information there will always be a similar reaction from someone in the audience. That's why I keep beating the drum, along with my frustrated observation of the gap between the myths and reality. I don't know anyone who works in a true meritocracy, but I know plenty of ambitious, well-educated women (many with offspring) who have found their career paths have differed significantly from their male peers and not just because of child bearing. They are good negotiators, idea generators and problem-solvers, and they have never been tempted to reflect male behaviour in a bid to fit in better because they recognise that's a hiding to nothing. Many of them are fed up with being told that they are good or bad mothers, and what they are doing wrong with their lives. We mums do tend to get blamed for a lot of social problems these days – from childhood obesity to spending too much time on Facebook. It's all our fault, particularly if we work outside the home, but as we've seen, Dads rarely cop the same type of criticism.

It's time for them to pitch in more, if the motherhood myth is to be effectively dismantled. It's a long way from Sydney Boys High to Silicon Valley, but Facebook's chief operating officer Sheryl Sandberg also did some of her own myth-busting at the TEDwomen conference in December 2010, where she spoke about how important it is to 'make sure your partner is a real partner'. On average, she said, women do two-thirds of the housework and three-quarters of the childcare. The answer starts with parity in the division of labour at home, because wives who shoulder more of the burden of childcare and housework than their husbands are more likely to lower their professional ambitions or drop out of the workforce altogether. She advises women to choose their life partners wisely, to make sure they will be supportive of their professional careers, and then make sure they keep striving for jobs they will love, especially before they have children.

> Once you have a child at home, your job better be really good to go back, because it's hard to leave that kid at home. And if two years ago you didn't take a promotion and some guy next to you did … you're going to be bored because you should have kept your foot on the gas pedal. Don't leave before you leave. Stay in, keep your foot on the gas pedal until the very day you need to leave to take a break for a child.

This message struck a chord and six months later her talk had been viewed more than 650 000 times. I can see why – apart from her message about partnership, Sandberg also stresses the need for women to sit at the table and lean in. Adding our tuppence worth is crucial. Ironically, Facebook has since come under fire for having no women at all on its board of seven. A lively campaign called 'Faceit' has been pressuring the company to better reflect its 65 per cent female users. This campaign, like 'Sack Vile Kyle', shows that women are more than willing to push for that input at the top table and, along with some judicious myth-busting, help to crack the glass ceiling. It's a conversation that should not be confined to women, but their experience needs to be well articulated or there will be a lot of wasted effort when the latest diversity program kicks off.

We would do so much better with switching to a new narrative if we had a crack at changing the rules of communication. Given there's still a need to explain why your surname is not the same as your husband's, it seems the anti-political correctness lobby efforts of recent years really struck a chord. As a writer, of course, the way we write and speak is a passion of mine, and it amazes me when I'm told not to be so petty about language because it 'doesn't really matter'. It does, and you only have to suggest that instead of referring to men you use women every so often to see how uncomfortable this makes many people. The language about women is in definite need of renovation and not just for the likes of Kyle Sandilands. On a practical level, I particularly like the advice feminist icon Gloria Steinem in The Women's Media Blog, on how journalists can avoid sexism in their coverage, because it makes clear the distinction between treating people equally and fairly (and is just as handy for those outside the media):

> The most workable definition of equality for journalists is reversibility. Don't mention her young children unless you would also mention his, or describe her clothes unless you would describe his, or say she's shrill or attractive unless the same adjectives would be applied to a man ... Don't say she has no professional training but he worked his way up. Don't ask her if she's running as a women's candidate unless you ask him if he's running as a men's candidate; ask both about the gender gap, the women's vote. By extension, don't say someone is a Muslim unless you also identify Christians and Jews, or identify only some people by race, ethnicity or sexuality and not others. However, this does NOT mean being even-handedly positive or negative when only one person or side has done something positive or negative. Equality allows accuracy.

Equality also allows differences to be acknowledged, but these should be based on accurate data too. There's plenty of work to do in dismantling the innate male versus female myth – it makes great headlines, but not great sense, as the analysis of myth 6 shows. It continues to feed many of the myths. There is little evidence to show that women are vastly different from men in everything from their brain structure to their levels of ambition, negotiating skills and reasons for wanting a good job. However, there is quite a lot of information to support the idea that there are very basic similarities in what is important to all of us, regardless of gender, and the business world needs to be reminded of that. Paradoxically, at the same time there's the reality that the problems women face, fed by these inaccurate and unhelpful assumptions, do result in their workplace experience being very different from their male colleagues.

But these variations are still interpreted by many in the business ranks as the result of 'choices', and often as a triumph of nature over nurture. There's a lack of appreciation that many of the so-called choices women make around jobs and family are not really about selecting from a range of viable options but are decisions constrained by context, social norms and, at a basic level, about who earns most and picks up the kids. Relying on a biologically determinist view of female lives continues to prop up classic gender stereotypes, and in the workplace is manifested in clinging to a male breadwinner model that is way out of date.

However, examining the evidence leaves us with a very different narrative than the one currently circulating, and importantly reveals a chasm between policy, practice and attitudes in most organisations. Closing that gap will require much more clarity about its real causes and the lack of success in changing the status quo. It will need clarity instead of confusion about the principles of affirmative action (which aims to provide extra assistance to those who fall behind), and the fact that equal opportunity doesn't mean treating everyone in the same way, blithely ignoring socially defined gender roles. Unpicking our myths shows how deeply the misunderstandings and, yes, resentment, can run when women are still seen to be intruders in the workplace, peripheral to the main game and getting more time off too (and less pay and status, but let's not get picky).

We now have plenty of proof that gender policies and targets and even pockets of goodwill in business are necessary but not sufficient. You can't change attitudes or shift behaviour only to trip over a range of biased processes – where selection criteria for a job or promotion favours a dominant group. Nor do a host of diversity programs add up to anything different if those in charge hold firmly to the mythologies about women and work. Responses to the problem in management ranks have typically wavered between dunking women into male leadership training (called the 'add women and stir' approach) or giving them a male makeover (fix the women). Both are ineffective and miss the point, as the evidence debunking the deficit myth shows.

This new story about gender and work is actually also about the future and optimism. Progress towards gender-balanced companies is a strategic economic issue that affects leadership, markets and talent, Wittenberg-Cox told me. Instead, conversations often concentrate on maternity leave or flexibility and that's what organisations think is the solution. While it satisfies some women in the short term, it can have a 'keep them happy and keep them down' effect, and the focus should be on reframing the issue and approaching it as a strategic business advantage. The companies doing better in this arena have one thing in common: it's all a question of CEOs and leadership, and that's the only real difference between companies that value the benefits of gender parity and those that don't, she said. These leaders understand that in many countries half the workforce and a growing number of their customers are female. But many in business are simply not facing the magnitude of the shift going on, and, Wittenberg-Cox points out, in Australia we are tinkering round with issues like boards when there's so much to do.

Not too long before I finished writing this book I was sitting in the Fairfax staff cafe in Sydney talking to consultant Deborah May about her work on gender and her recent research into the issue at the Treasury (see myth 7). I mentioned my book and the myths, and she said one of the reasons they continued to be circulated in senior ranks – which is where organisational settings and norms about what's acceptable are formed – is probably to do with the unrealistic pressure on these people to know all the answers. The gender stuff is an area they simply haven't thought much about, or their home situation has lulled them into thinking there is no problem any more. As a result there's a temptation to default to conjecture and generalisations without real evidence or even analysis. Later the same day I interviewed Deloitte partner Lisa Barry about the notion of lateral careers that can replace the classic ladder model in most businesses. She commented that many senior groups in Australian corporates – men and women – were not very interested in changing the dynamics of traditional hierarchies, because these mechanisms had served them well, allowing them to rise to the top. Both women's incisive comments reminded me that vested interests have helped to keep the myths buoyant and current.

It is also clear to me there's a self-reinforcing element to many of the myths that makes them that bit more frustratingly tricky to debunk. Women do play a role in perpetuating the myths that I have examined. It's only to be expected when women are in fact absorbing the many assumptions made about their gender. As Cordelia Fine points out in 'Status quota', 'As a large body of research shows, cultural realities and beliefs about females and males – represented in existing inequalities, in media, and in the minds, expectations and behaviour of others as well as our own – alter our social perceptions, self-concepts, interests and behaviours'.

I've written a lot about assumptions made by some men about women throughout this book, but it's just as damaging to think that all women have the same views about gender equity or even find the topic to be of interest. It's just like talking about the women's vote – what exactly does that mean? Does half the population vote en masse? Some women have very different views from mine and are very critical of women's networks or diversity programs. Many women also resist the idea of quotas or targets for women. As critical as I am of some measures – traditional mentoring, unconscious bias seminars – I still believe the sum of the parts is important and with more sophisticated debate, and better information and understanding we can all have our say and more effectively make some headway.

If we don't work out how to challenge the myths

and talk about fairness, equality and difference, the smug defence of business as usual will continue to reproduce more mythology in the workplace. There's a growing need to dismantle the notion that the political is now the personal (to reverse Gloria Steinem's famous quote). This is not about creating victims but liberating women by helping them to understand that the barriers they face are shared. That kind of realisation can break a cycle of paralysis that many women fall into when they are encouraged to believe they made the wrong choices all along.

When the 100th anniversary of International Women's Day was celebrated in 2011 I wrote another list for the column (if you're on a good thing ...). Some of it was reminiscent of the 7 myths, but it was also a direct call to action 100 years after women mobilised to gain the right to vote. Here it is with some additions:

1   *Promote more women* It doesn't sound like a big ask, but it surely has taken a long time to get those ratios changed at the top. And, sadly, Australia's listed companies have registered a decline in the number of women at the most senior levels over recent years. This can and must be reversed. The impact of heavily male-dominated management ranks on the younger generations of women emerging from schools and universities into the workforce

is not exactly motivating. You can't be what you can't see. Aspiring women entering most businesses in Australia today are being sent a clear message: senior jobs are not for you. There's no easy fix here, but recognition that the deck is stacked against women gives some clues.

2   *Close the pay gap* The avalanche of data on the widening gender pay gap has not as yet translated to much action, and this has to be a higher priority. Business has all kinds of checks and balances to ensure people are treated properly – so add this to the list. Appropriate recognition and reward should be a given to all employees, not as a favour. Pay audits and regular attention to pay scales and job evaluation can be introduced to help to ensure this problem is addressed.

3   *Share the domestic labour* Women are still shouldering 80 per cent of house and caring work, but an ever-increasing number are in paid work. That's not an equitable or sustainable equation. It's time to share and the barriers to entry are very low. Anyone can tidy up, pick up kids or clean the toilet. The days of leaving the domestic load on one set of shoulders is long gone.

4   *Eradicate double standards* Easier said than

done, but a bit more thought about what we expect from women in the workplace, and not from men, would help – and vice-versa. Don't tell women to toughen up, then punish them for being aggressive. Don't tell women they are their own worst enemies, then reward men for playing politics. Don't ask a woman who has just been promoted how she'll manage to see enough of her children. Don't compliment the fathers who leave early to do the school pick-up and sneer at women who do the same. Don't set higher standards for women and then expect gratitude.

5   *Normalise women as breadwinners* Given that close to 60 per cent of Australian women are wage earners and the number is steadily increasing, there should be little doubt they are working for more than pin money. But many workplaces still reflect an old-fashioned idea that women are discretionary workers without bills to pay. Get over that misconception and many other negative assumptions may begin to lose currency.

6   *Bring back equity as an argument* Fairness is actually the most important reason for gender equity. Half the population is not a special interest group, nor do women magically transform business results. A mixture of people

in the top team of an organisation reflects a true meritocracy. But most of all, the fairness test reminds us of the staggeringly obvious: women are not special or set apart, but members of society with all the rights and obligations that entails. And let's remember that International Women's Day is about women supporting each other, and despite plenty of negative stereotyping, that's actually something most of us do rather well.

So where does that leave us? If every one of the myths was effectively busted would we have a nirvana for women in the workplace? Probably not. We are humans, after all, and history gives us a pretty good sense that confronting strong beliefs and social norms is a lengthy and imperfect process. There's lots of collateral damage from forcing such change, with unintended consequences too. Nevertheless, it is often said that shifting attitudes is extremely difficult, but you can change behaviour in a workplace and challenging the 7 myths can help show where we can all start. Just like being a feminist, this doesn't require joining a club, attending rallies or writing an action plan. Nor does it set up unrealistic expectations that there is a single response, silver bullet, or foolproof way to solve these problems. It's a chance for some more informed conversations and maybe, occasionally, changing someone's mind.

I read recently that if the current rate of change continued, gender parity – 50/50 representation – would take another 160 years to achieve in Australia. Hopefully white-anting some of the myths will shave a few decades off that and we will not leave them hanging around for our daughters to face.

REFERENCES

Auletta, K 2011, 'A woman's place', *The New Yorker*, 11 July.

Australian Human Rights Commission 2010, *Gender Equality Blueprint*, AHRC, Sydney.

Belkin, L 2003, 'The opt-out revolution', *The New York Times Magazine*, 26 October.

Beyond the Spin 2010, *The 100 Percent Project*, Issue 1, Autumn.

Boushey H 2005, 'Are women opting out? Debunking the myth', briefing paper, Center for Economic and Policy Research, Washington DC, November.

Carter, N & Silva C 2011, *The Myth of the Ideal Worker: Does doing all the right things get women ahead?* Catalyst at www.catalyst.org/publication/509/the-myth-of-the-ideal-worker-does-doing-all-the-right-things-really-get-women-ahead

Carter N & Silva C 2010, *The Pipeline's Broken Promise*, Catalyst.

Cassells, R, Miranti, R, Nepal B & Tanton, R 2009 *She Works Hard For The Money: Australian Women and the Gender Divide,* NATSEM/AMP, University of Canberra, no. 22, April.

CEDA 2011, *Understanding the Gender Pay Gap: Looking Below the Surface,* CEDA, September. Viewed 4 May 2012 at www.ceda.com.au/media/143387/wilsept21.pdf

Cochrane, K 2011, 'Why is British life dominated by men?' *The Guardian*, 5 December.

Coffman, J & Hagey, R 2010, *Flexible Work Models:*

How to Bring Sustainability to a 24/7 World. Bain & Company.

Corporations and Markets Advisory Committee 2009, *Diversity on Boards of Directors:* Report, CAMAC, March.

Correll S & Benard S 2007, 'Getting a job: Is there a motherhood penalty?' *American Journal of Sociology,* no. 112, pp. 1297–338.

Ely, R, Ibarra, H & Kolb, D 2011, *Taking Gender into Account: Theory and Design for Women's Leadership Programs,* INSEAD Working Paper. Viewed 1 May 2012 at www.insead.edu/facultyresearch/research/doc. cfm?did=48085

EOWA 2010 *Australian Census of Women in Leadership 2008–2010,* Australian Government. Viewed 1 May 2012 at www.eowa.gov.au/Australian_Women_In_ Leadership_Census.asp

EOWA 2008, *Survey on Workplace Flexibility,* Equal Opportunity for Women in the Workforce Agency.

EOWA, 2008, *Generation F.* Viewed 2 May 2012 at www. eowa.gov.au/Information_Centres/Resource_Centre/ EOWA_Publications/Generation_F/Documents/ GENERATION_F.pdf

EOWA/Diversity Council 2008, 'Understanding the gender pay gap', fact sheet. Viewed 1 May 2012 at www. eowa.gov.au/Pay_Equity/Pay_Equity_Information/ Understanding_the_gap.pdf

FaHCSIA 2010, 'Improving Women's Economic Wellbeing', July. Accessed 3 May 2012 at www.fahcsia.gov.au/sa/ women/pubs/general/factsheet_women_issues/Pages/ facts3.aspx

Fels, A 2005, *Necessary Dreams: Ambition in Women's Changing Lives,* Pantheon Books.

Fels, A 2004, 'Do women lack ambition?' *Harvard Business Review,* April.

Financial Services Institute of Australasia 2010, *Bridging the Gender Divide*, Finsia.

Fine, C 2012, 'Status quota: Do mandatory gender quotas work?' *The Monthly*, March.

Fine, C 2010, *Delusions of Gender: How our Minds, Society and Neurosexism Create Difference*, Icon.

Flynn, J, Heath, K & Davis Holt, M 2011, 'Four ways women stunt their careers unintentionally', *Harvard Business Review*, 20 October.

Fox, C 2012, 'Mother Lode', *Financial Review Boss*, 9 March.

Fox, C 2011, 'Law firm proves that real change is possible', *Financial Review*, 15 November.

Fox, C, 2010, 'Time to get creative about finding female talent', *Financial Review*, 2 March.

Fox, C 2009, 'Award winners show the way in closing the gap', *Financial Review*, 17 November.

Fox, C 2009, 'The McPremium', *Financial Review Boss*, 9 October.

Fox, C & Hooper, N, 2011, 'New men define path to productive economy', *Financial Review*, 13 October.

Fox, C & Hooper, N, 2010, 'The smart curve: How to get more women in top jobs', *Financial Review Boss*, 19 January.

Frankel L & Frohlinger, C 2011, *Nice Girls Just Don't Get It*, Crown Publishing.

Goldin, C, Katz, L F, Hausman, N & Ward B 2008, *Harvard and Beyond Project*, April. Viewed 1 May 2012 at www.economics.harvard.edu/faculty/goldin/harvardandbeyond

Goldman Sachs JBWere, 2009, *Australia's Hidden Resource: The Economic Case for Increasing Female Participation*, Research report, 26 November.

Groysberg, B 2008, 'How star women build portable skills', *Harvard Business Review*, February.

Grufferman, B H 2011, 'What Post-50 Americans fear most … and why', *The Huffington Post*, blog, 20 December.

Gudrais, E 2010, 'Family or fortune', *Harvard magazine*, Jan–Feb. Viewed 2 May 2012 at harvardmagazine.com/2010/01/family-or-fortune

Guinness, M 2011, 'Is this the world's sexiest woman?' *The Guardian*, 17 July.

Haslam, S A, Ryan, M K, Kulich, C, Trojanowski, G & Atkins, C 2010, 'Investing with prejudice: The relationship between women's presence on company boards and objective and subjective measures of company performance', *British Journal of Management* vol. 21, no. 2, pp. 484–97, June.

Hastie, C 2006, *Exploring Horizontal Violence*, MIDIRS at http://scu-au.academia.edu/CarolynHastie/Papers/497411/Exploring_Horizontal_Violence

Heffernan, M 2011, *Wilful Blindness*, Simon & Schuster.

Horin A 2012, 'White-collar men facing age discrimination', *Sydney Morning Herald,* 30 January.

House Standing Committee on Employment and Workplace Relations 2009, *Making it Fair* Australian Government. Viewed 3 May 2012 at www.aph.gov.au/house/committee/ewr/payequity/report.htm

Howard A 2009, *Holding Women Back: Troubling Discoveries and Best Practices for Helping Female Leaders Succeed*, DDI Consulting.

Hrdlicka, J, Cottrell, D & Sanders, M 2010, *Level the Playing Field: A Call for Action on Gender Parity in Australia,* Bain & Company, September.

Institute of Leadership & Management 2011, *Ambition and Gender at Work*, Institute of Leadership & Management, London, UK.

Jordan-Young, R 2010, *Brain Storm: The Flaws in the Science of Sex Differences*, Harvard University Press, Cambridge, MA.

Joy, L & Carter N 2007, 'The bottom line: Corporate performance and women's representation on boards', *Catalyst*, October Viewed 5 May at www.catalyst.org/publication/200/the-bottom-line-corporate-performance-and-womens-representation-on-boards

Kee, H J 2006 'Glass ceiling or sticky floor? Exploring the Australian gender pay gap', *Economic Record*, vol. 82, No. 259, pp. 408–27, December.

Kelly, S 2009, *Don't Stop Thinking About Tomorrow: The Changing Face of Retirement – the Past, the Present and the Future*, NATSEM/AMP, University of Canberra, no. 24, November.

Klein P 2011, When will women become equal on boards? *Forbes,* The CSR blog, 27 June.

Koenig, A M, Eagly, A, Mitchell, A A & Ristikari, T 2011, 'Are leader stereotypes masculine? A meta-analysis of three research paradigms', *Psychological Bulletin,* July, 137, pp. 616–42.

Kulich, C, Trojanowski G, Ryan, M, Haslam, A & Renneboog, L 2010, 'Who gets the carrot and who gets the stick? Evidence of gender disparities in executive remuneration', *Strategic Management Journal*, vol. 321, July, pp. 301–21.

Kurtulus F A & Tomaskovic-Devey, D 2012,' Do female top managers help women to advance? A panel study using EE0-1 records', *The ANNALS of the American Academy of Political and Social Science* no. 639, pp. 173–97.

Leonhardt, D 2009, 'Work–life balance is especially difficult in finance', *New York Times,* 26 May.

Livermore, T, Rodgers, J R & Siminski, P 2009, 'The effect of motherhood on wages and wage growth: Evidence for Australia', PhD thesis.

Male Champions of Change 2011, *Our Experiences in Elevating the Representation of Women in Leadership:*

A letter from business leaders, October, Australian Human Rights Commission.

McCredie, J 2011, *Making Girls and Boys*, New South Books, Sydney.

McKinsey & Company, 2010, *Moving Women to the Top: McKinsey Global Survey Results*.

McKinsey & Company 2010, *Women at the Top of Corporations: Making it Happen*, Women Matter report.

McKinsey & Company 2007, *Women Matter: Gender Diversity, a Corporate Performance Driver*.

Media Research Group 2012, *Women in Media: Media Coverage Analysis of Prominent Female Spokespeople across Metropolitan Print Media*, March.

Moran, C 2011, *How to be a Woman*, Ebury Press.

Morley, K 2010, *Unlocking the Potential of Women at Work: A Decade of Evidence*, White Paper, Gender Worx.

Moss, S 2008, 'Social dominance theory', *Psychlopedia*, December.

Pinto C & Williams, J 2012, 'Hidden gender bias in the workplace', *HR Management*, February.

Piterman, H 2011, *Women in Leadership: Looking Below the Surface*, CEDA report.

Piterman, H 2008, *The Leadership Challenge: Women in Management*. Viewed 1 May 2012 at www.fahcsia. gov.au/sa/women/pubs/economic/leadership_challenge_ women_manage/Documents/report_march08.pdf

Pocock, B, Skinner, N, & Ichii, R 2010, *Work, Life and Workplace Flexibility: The Australian Work and Life Index 2009*, AWALI, University of South Australia.

Pocock, B, Skinner, N & Williams, P 2012, *Time Bomb: Work, Rest and Play in Australia Today*, New South Books, Sydney.

Prime, J, Moss-Racusin, C-A & Foust-Cummings, H 2009,

'Engaging men in gender initiatives', *Catalyst*, New York, December.

Reibey Institute, 2010–11, *ASX 500 – Women Leaders: Preliminary Research Note,* Reibey Institute, Riverview NSW.

Rodgers-Healey, D 2009, *Women Getting into Boards,* Australian Centre for Leadership for Women.

Ryan, M K, & Haslam, S A 2005, 'The glass cliff: Evidence that women that women are over-represented in precarious leadership positions', *British Journal of Management*, 16, pp. 81–90.

Sandberg, S 2010, 'Why we have too few women leaders', TED Talks, December.

Sanders, M, Hrdlicka, J, Hellicar, M, Cottrell, D & Knox, J 2011, 'What stops women from reaching the top? Confronting the tough issues', Bain & Company, Chief Executive Women. Viewed 4 May 2012 at www.bain.com/offices/australia/en_us/publications/what-stops-women-from-reaching-the-top.aspx

Skenazy, L 2009, *Free Range Kids*, Jossey-Bass, San Francisco.

Steinem, G 2010, 'Statement on equality', Women's Media Center blog, 31 August.

Swan, J 2012, '"Sack Vile Kyle" campaign drives sponsors away', *Sydney Morning Herald,* 20 January.

The 100% Project 2011, *Men at Work: What They Want and Why it Matters for Women.*

Tropea, K, de Cieri, H & Sheehan, C 2010 'Quotas on boards?' *Beyond the Spin*, Winter 2010.

University of New South Wales, 2011, *If men are not slackers why are women still holding the baby?* Knowledge@Australian School of Business, 13 September.

Watson, I 2010, 'Decomposing the gender pay gap in the Australian managerial labour market', *Australian*

Journal of Labour Economics, vol. 13, no. 1, pp. 49–79.

Wittenberg-Cox A 2012, 'Corporate leadership is still all about the boys', *Harvard Business Review* blog, 16 February.

Wittenberg-Cox A 2010, 'Why focusing on the gender pay gap misses the point', *Harvard Business Review* Blog, 12 April 2010.

Wittenberg-Cox, A 2008, *Why Women Mean Business: Understanding the Emergence of Our next Economic Revolution*, Jossey-Bass, San Francisco.

Woolley A & Malone T 2011, 'What makes a team smarter? More women', *Harvard Business Review*, June.

Wright, N 2012, *Attitudes to Older Workers*, Financial Services Council, Sydney, January, viewed 4 May 2012 at www.fsc.org.au/downloads/uploaded/2012_3001_older%20workers_report_4464.pdf

INDEX